PRENTICE—HALL
FOUNDATIONS OF MODERN SOCIOLOGY SERIES
Alex Inkeles, Editor

INDUSTRIAL SOCIOLOGY
Ivar Berg

DEVIANCE AND CONTROL
Albert K. Cohen

MODERN ORGANIZATIONS
Amitai Etzioni

SOCIAL PROBLEMS
Amitai Etzioni

LAW AND SOCIETY: An Introduction
Lawrence M. Friedman

THE FAMILY
William J. Goode

SOCIETY AND POPULATION, Second Edition
David M. Heer

WHAT IS SOCIOLOGY? An Introduction to the Discipline and Profession
Alex Inkeles

THE SOCIOLOGY OF SMALL GROUPS
Theodore M. Mills

SOCIAL CHANGE, Second Edition
Wilbert E. Moore

THE SOCIOLOGY OF RELIGION
Thomas F. O'Dea

THE EVOLUTION OF SOCIETIES
Talcott Parsons

RURAL SOCIETY
Irwin T. Sanders

THE AMERICAN SCHOOL: A Sociological Analysis
Patricia C. Sexton

THE SOCIOLOGY OF ECONOMIC LIFE, Second Edition
Neil J. Smelser

FOUNDATIONS OF MODERN SOCIOLOGY, Second Edition
Metta Spencer

SOCIAL STRATIFICATION: The Forms and Functions of Inequality
Melvin M. Tumin

Foundations of Modern Sociology Series

modern
organizations

Amitai Etzioni, *Columbia University*

 PRENTICE HALL, Englewood Cliffs, NJ 07632

Library of Congress Catalog No.: 64-17073

Designed by Harry Rinehart

Prentice-Hall Foundations of Modern Sociology Series

Alex Inkeles, *Editor*

Printed in the United States of America

40   39   38   37   36   35   34

ISBN 0-13-596049-5

Prentice-Hall International (UK) Limited, *London*
Prentice-Hall of Australia Pty. Limited, *Sydney*
Prentice-Hall Canada Inc., *Toronto*
Prentice-Hall Hispanoamericana, S.A., *Mexico*
Prentice-Hall of India Private Limited, *New Delhi*
Prentice-Hall of Japan, Inc., *Tokyo*
Simon & Schuster Asia Pte. Ltd., *Singapore*
Editora Prentice-Hall do Brasil, Ltda., *Rio de Janeiro*

contents

vi

contents

rationality
and happiness:
the organizational
dilemma

one

Our society is an organizational society.[1] We are born in organizations, educated by organizations, and most of us spend much of our lives working for organizations. We spend much of our leisure time paying, playing, and praying in organizations. Most of us will die in an organization, and when the time comes for burial, the largest organization of all—the state—must grant official permission.

In contrast to earlier societies, modern society has placed a high moral value on rationality, effectiveness, and efficiency. Modern civilization depends largely on organizations as the most rational and efficient form of social grouping known. By coordinating a large number of human actions, the organization creates a powerful social tool. It combines its personnel with its resources, weaving together leaders, experts, workers, machines, and raw materials. At the same time it continually evaluates how well it is performing and tries to adjust itself accordingly in order to achieve its goals. As we shall see, all this allows organizations to serve the various needs of society and its citizens more efficiently than smaller and more natural human groupings, such as families, friendship groups, and communities.

Organizations are not a modern invention. The Pharaohs used organizations to build the pyramids. The emperors of China used organizations a thousand years ago to construct great irrigation systems. And the first Popes created a universal church to serve a world religion. Modern society, how-

[1] Robert Presthus, *The Organizational Society* (New York: Knopf, 1962).

1

ever, has more organizations, these fulfilling a greater variety of societal and personal needs, involving a greater proportion of its citizens, and affecting a larger segment of their lives. In fact, modern society has so many organizations that a whole set of second-order organizations is needed to organize and supervise organizations. In the United States, such regulatory commissions as the Securities and Exchange Commission and the National Labor Relations Board are examples.

Finally we can also say that the modern organization is generally more efficient than the ancient or medieval species. Changes in the nature of society have made the social environment more congenial to organizations, and the art of planning, coordinating, and controlling has developed with the study of administration.

This increase in the scope and rationality of organizations has not come without social and human cost. Many people who work for organizations are deeply frustrated and alienated from their work. The organization, instead of being society's obedient servant, sometimes becomes its master. Modern society—far from being a *Gemeinschaft* town meeting—often seems closer to a battleground where organizational giants clash. But it is widely agreed that the undesirable side effects do not outweigh the considerable benefits of organizations. Although few people would agree to return to a more traditional society where human groupings were small, intimate, and inefficient, constant efforts are being made to reduce the frustrating and distorting side effects of these huge social instruments of modern society, while maintaining, even enhancing, their efficacy.

At this point we must confront a major misunderstanding. *Not* all that enhances rationality reduces happiness, and *not* all that increases happiness reduces efficiency. Human resources are among the major means used by the organization to achieve its goals. Generally the less the organization alienates its personnel, the more efficient it is. Satisfied workers usually work harder and better than frustrated ones. Within limits, happiness heightens efficiency in organizations and, conversely, without efficient organizations much of our happiness is unthinkable. Without well-run organizations our standard of living, our level of culture, and our democratic life could not be maintained. Thus, to a degree, *organizational rationality and human happiness go hand in hand*. But a point is reached in every organization where happiness and efficiency cease to support each other. Not all work can be well-paid or gratifying, and not all regulations and orders can be made acceptable. Here we face a true dilemma.

The problem of modern organizations is thus how to construct human groupings that are as rational as possible, and at the same time produce a minimum of undesirable side effects and a maximum of satisfaction. We find both a record of progress and setbacks in the search for the best combination of these human values. As we shall see, this record is marked by conflicting opinions among various experts and "schools" as how best to coordinate human efforts in the service of organizational goals.

2

rationality and happiness: the organizational dilemma

Organizations Defined

Organizations are social units (or human groupings) deliberately constructed and reconstructed to seek specific goals.[2] Corporations, armies, schools, hospitals, churches, and prisons are included; tribes, classes, ethnic groups, friendship groups, and families are excluded. Organizations are characterized by: (1) divisions of labor, power, and communication responsibilities, divisions which are not random or traditionally patterned, but deliberately planned to enhance the realization of specific goals; (2) the presence of one or more power centers which control the concerted efforts of the organization and direct them toward its goals; these power centers also must review continuously the organization's performance and re-pattern its structure, where necessary, to increase its efficiency; (3) substitution of personnel, i.e., unsatisfactory persons can be removed and others assigned their tasks. The organization can also recombine its personnel through transfer and promotion.

Other social units are marked by some degree of conscious planning (e.g., the family budget), by the existence of power centers (e.g., tribal chiefs), and by replaceable membership (e.g., through divorce), but the extent to which these other social units are consciously planned, deliberately structured and restructured, with a membership which is routinely changed, is much less than in the case of those social units we are calling *organizations*. Hence organizations are much more in control of their nature and destiny than any other social grouping.

There are many synonyms for the term, *organization*. One, *bureaucracy*, has two disadvantages. First, *bureaucracy* often carries a negative connotation for the layman, while *organization* is a neutral term. Second, *bureaucracy* implies for those familiar with Weber's work (see Chapter 5) that the unit is organized according to the principles he specified. But many organizations, including many modern ones, are not bureaucratic in this technical sense. Hospitals, for instance, do not have one center of decision-making, whereas bureaucracies do, by definition. *Formal organization* refers to one set of characteristics of organizations. We discuss this aspect below; here it suffices to say that this term does not refer to an organization as an entity, but only to a part of it. *Institution* is sometimes used to refer to certain types of organizations, either quite respectable ones as in "GM is an institution," or quite unrespectable ones, as in "He is in an institution." Sometimes institution refers to a quite different phenomenon—namely, to a normative principle that culturally defines behavior such as marriage or property. Because of these two conflicting usages, this term has probably caused more confusion than *formal organization* and *bureaucracy* together. All three might well be avoided in favor of the simple term, *organization*.

Since many social groupings have some degree of patterning and some control structure—e.g., in contrast to a mob—*social organization* has been

---

[2] Talcott Parsons, *Structure and Process in Modern Societies* (Glencoe, Ill.: The Free Press, 1960), p. 17. Some minimal amount of such construction and reconstruction will be found in all social units, but it is much higher in organizations.

rationality and happiness: the organizational dilemma

used to characterize these phenomena. But in recent years *social structure* has been increasingly employed to describe these characteristics of social units. Thus we can safely reserve the term *organizations* to refer to planned units, deliberately structured for the purpose of attaining specific goals, and do without social organizations altogether.

The Plan of the Book

The plan of this book follows our definition of organizations as social units that pursue specific goals which they are structured to serve, obviously under some social circumstances. Therefore the book has three foci: organizational goals; organizational structure; and organizations and their social environment. Considerably more space is devoted to organizational structure than to the other topics, for two reasons: First, more research has been conducted and more writings are available on organizational structure than on organizational goals (Chapter 2) and environment. Second, the major schools of organizational analysis have fixed their interests on structural aspects of the organization, and thus, we may best evaluate these different approaches in the context of organizational structure.

The approach to organizational structure used here can be viewed as a synthesis of two schools—the *formal*, Scientific Management school and the *informal*, Human Relations school, whose major contributions are analyzed in Chapters 3 and 4, respectively. The emerging synthesis—the Structuralist approach—combines the formal and informal perspectives as well as other aspects of organizational analysis (Chapter 4). There follows in Chapter 5 a presentation of Max Weber's theory of bureaucracy, which represents the work of an early Structuralist, and which is of great importance in itself. The rest of the volume applies the Structuralist approach to the study of organizational structure from a comparative perspective (Chapters 6–8), to an examination of the relations of organizations to their clients (Chapter 9), and to the larger environment (Chapter 10).

rationality and happiness: the organizational dilemma

the organization goal: master or servant?

two

The goals of organizations serve many functions. They provide orientation by depicting a future state of affairs which the organization strives to realize. Thus they set down guide lines for organizational activity. Goals also constitute a source of legitimacy which justifies the activities of an organization and, indeed, its very existence. Moreover goals serve as standards by which members of an organization and outsiders can assess the success of the organization—i.e., its effectiveness and efficiency. Goals also serve in a similar fashion as measuring rods for the student of organizations who tries to determine how well the organization is doing.

Organizations are social units which pursue specific goals; their very *raison d'etre* is the service of these goals. But once formed, organizations acquire their own needs, these sometimes becoming the masters of the organization. This happens, for example, when a fund-raising organization spends more money on staff, buildings, and publicity than on the charity itself, for which funds are raised. In such instances, organizations reduce the service to their initial goals in order to satisfy their acquired needs, rather than adjust the service of their acquired needs to that of their goals. Sometimes organizations go so far as to abandon their initial goals and pursue new ones more suited to the organization's needs. This is what we mean when we say that the organizational goal becomes the servant of the organization rather than its master. In this chapter we consider the questions: What are organizational goals? Under what conditions can they be met? When do the organizational needs become masters, subverting the

5

initial goals? How are organizational effectiveness and efficiency defined, and what organizational problem does their very measurement raise? The chapter closes with a discussion of the danger of using goals as the prime tool for studying and evaluating an organization, and a suggested alternative.

The Nature
of Organizational Goals

An organizational goal is a desired state of affairs which the organization attempts to realize. The organization may or may not be able to bring about this desired image of the future. But if the goal is reached, it ceases to be a guiding image for the organization and is assimilated to the organization or its environment. For example, the establishing of a Jewish state was the goal of the Zionist movement. In 1948, when this goal became a reality, it ceased to be a desired goal. In this sense a goal never exists; it is a state which we seek, not one we have. Such future states of affairs, though images, have a very real sociological force that affects contemporary actions and reactions.

But whose image of the future does the organization pursue? That of top executives? The board of directors or trustees? The majority of the members? Actually none of these. The organizational goal is that future state of affairs which the organization as a collectivity is trying to bring about. It is in part affected by the goals of the top executives, those of the board of directors, and those of the rank and file. It is determined sometimes in a peaceful consultation, sometimes in a power play among the various organizational divisions, plants, cabals, ranks, and "personalities."

How then does one determine what is the goal of an organization? In part the participants may act as informants. We may interview executives and employees of various departments to establish what they see as the organization's goals. In interviewing them, we must carefully distinguish their personal goals from the goals of the collectivity. An executive's goal might be to gain a larger stock option; that of the finance department, to balance the budget; the employees', to gain a raise. Still all might view the organizational goal as making a profit. Profit-making might be selected because they believe that it is the way for them to fulfill their personal or departmental goals, or because they believe in principle that a private enterprise should make profit. In either case their goals should not be confused with the organizational ones. The participants should be specifically asked what they see as the organizational goal, as distinct from their own or from those which they think the organization *ought* to pursue. We may also get relevant information by studying minutes of the board meetings and by examining other documents of the organization. We can also analyze the division of labor of the organization, its flow of work, and its allocation of resources as reflected in its budget to determine the actual organization's orientation to a future state of affairs.

Especially revealing are those situations in which the distribution of manpower and material resources clearly suggests a direction of effort different from that expressed by the informants. For instance, if the administrator of a mental hospital informs us that his hospital is in the business

6

the organization goal: master or servant?

of curing people, and we find that there are but 4 doctors (only one of whom has had psychiatric training) serving 5,000 patients, that the hospital aides have no more training or interest in therapy than prison guards, that 90 per cent of the patients—many of them suffering from senility which is generally considered incurable—have spent 10 years or more in the hospital, then we might infer that the hospital's goal is to keep the level of public disturbance down or to care for the aged, but not to cure or rehabilitate.

There are at least two reasons why the head of an organization might maintain that the organization is seeking certain goals which in fact differ from the ones it actually pursues. In some instances the head may be unaware of the discrepancy; the true situation is hidden from him. The heads of some university departments, for instance, have only very inaccurate information on what happens to most of their "product," the graduates. Thus a department head and his staff might believe that the department is devoted to training future Nobel Prize winners in physics, while in practice it operates mainly to provide the electronics industry with fairly capable applied researchers. More commonly, organizational leaders quite consciously express goals which differ from those actually pursued because such masking will serve the goals the organization actually pursues. Thus an organization whose real goal is to make a profit might benefit if it can pass as an educational, non-profit organization. And an organization whose goal is to overthrow the legitimate government of a country is likely to benefit if it can pass as a legitimate political party.

The researcher will define as the *real goals* of the organization those future states toward which a majority of the organization's means and the major organizational commitments of the participants are directed, and which, in cases of conflict with goals which are *stated* but command few resources, have clear priority. Sometimes establishing intimate contact with key participants allows the researcher to determine how aware informants are of any discrepancy between real and stated goals. Generally, however, it is unwise to depend entirely on interviews for information on an organization's real goals. An examination of the allocation of resources and direction of efforts is often a necessary complementary research method for obtaining satisfactory results.

The distinction between real and stated goals should not be confused with the important difference between intended and unintended consequences widely used in sociology. Goals are always intended; the difference is between stated intentions and real ones. Unintended consequences are strictly unplanned, unexpected results of action oriented toward some goal.

How Goals Are Set

Virtually all organizations have a formal, explicitly recognized, sometimes legally specified organ for setting the initial goals and for their amendment. In some organizations goals are set formally by a vote of the stockholders; in others, by a vote of the members (e.g., in some labor unions); in still others, by a small number of trustees; and in a few by an individual who owns and runs the organization

In practice, goals are often set in a complicated power play involving

7

various individuals and groups within and without the organization, and by reference to values which govern behavior in general and the specific behavior of the relevant individuals and groups in a particular society.

The following example, drawn from a well-known novel, illustrates the process by which goals may be set in an organization. In a furniture factory the young, idealistic head of the production department favors producing furniture of solid quality; the older head of the finance department is more interested in increasing profit by manufacturing furniture of lower quality. In part their differences reflect a power struggle between the two for the presidency of the corporation. Note that both find it necessary to appeal to general values—profit and quality—in their fight. Moreover the young production man is so committed to the reputation of the firm and the quality value that he would sooner make no profit than sacrifice this goal. The formal resolution of this conflict comes in the board of directors' meeting —although the main power struggle and maneuvering have ended.

There are many factors that enter into the struggle to determine an organization's goal or goals. Organizational departments or divisions often play a prominent role in the process. Personalities are another important determinant. When a strong leader has established himself in the key position of president or executive-director, it is frequently just as hard to unseat him, or to push through an organizational strategy to which he objects, as it is to run against the incumbent president of the United States, unless he commits a major blunder.

In addition to departments and personalities an important role is played by environmental forces. Most organizations are less autonomous than first seems to be the case. Consider a prison which will drastically reduce its security precautions if it carries out its plan to allow inmates to work in the fields, a measure deemed helpful in the shift from the goal of custody (keep them in) to that of rehabilitation (change them while they are in). The surrounding community will often object strongly, especially after an escape, to such a relaxation of security measures, and exerts considerable political pressure to prevent a change of the prison's goal from custodial to rehabilitative. If necessary, the community is willing to have the warden and staff of the prison removed. Similarly anti-trust laws, the Department of Health, labor unions, and other environmental forces set limits not only on the means an organization may use, but on the goals it may pursue.

Effectiveness, Efficiency, and the Danger of "Over-measurement"

Organizations are constructed to be the most effective and efficient social units. The actual *effectiveness* of a specific organization is determined by the degree to which it realizes its goals. The *efficiency* of an organization is measured by the amount of resources used to produce a unit of output. Output is usually closely related to, but not identical with, the organizational goals. For instance, Ford produces automobiles (its output), but its goal seems to be profit-making. The unit of output is a measurable quantity of whatever the organization may be producing, expressed in terms of automobiles, well patients, or what not. Efficiency increases as

8

the costs (resources used) decrease. Both current costs and changes in capital have to be taken into account.

It is important to note that while efficiency and effectiveness tend to go hand in hand, they not always do. An efficient company might make no profits, perhaps because of a declining market, and an inefficient one may return a high profit, because of a rising market. Moreover over-concern with efficiency may limit the scope of activities of an organization, while effectiveness might require a large variety of activities.

Measuring effectiveness and efficiency raises several thorny problems. When an organization has a goal which is limited and concrete, it is comparatively easy to measure effectiveness. For instance, in the case of two organizations—one whose goal was constructing a canal linking the Red and Mediterranean Seas and the other whose goal was building a tunnel between France and Britain—it is clear that the former was effective while the latter was not. If the organizational goal is a continuous one, measurement is already more difficult. If the purpose of a corporation is to make profit, and it makes 3 per cent one year, 4 the next year, and no profit the third, how effective is it? Here one must specify a standard, such as "Profit compared to that of similar corporations in the same period," in order to measure effectiveness. Finally, when we come to organizations whose output is not material (e.g., churches), statements about effectiveness are extremely difficult to validate.

The same problem attends measuring efficiency and such related concepts as output, productivity, and costs. It is possible to determine how much it costs to make a car in one factory as against another (although even here there are some tricky problems, such as measuring amortization of the capital equipment and changes in the morale of the workers). But when it comes to comparing the efficiency of two hospitals (sometimes measured by costs per bed), or of two schools (rarely measured by serious students of organization), the concept becomes considerably more vague; one hospital or school or church is more efficient than another only if it produces the *same* product at a lower cost, and this "sameness" is a very difficult thing to establish.

Most organizations under pressure to be rational are eager to measure their efficiency. Curiously, the very effort—the desire to establish how we are doing and to find ways of improving if we are not doing as well as we ought to do—often has quite undesired effects from the point of view of the organizational goals. Frequent measuring can distort the organizational efforts because, as a rule, some aspects of its output are more measurable than the others. Frequent measuring tends to encourage over-production of highly measurable items and neglect of the less measurable ones. When a factory puts great pressure on its production people to increase their efficiency, they might well produce more items but of a lower quality. If quality control is then tightened, the production people might neglect the maintenance of their equipment to put more efforts into satisfying the increased pressure to maintain quality.

The distortion consequences of over-measuring are larger when it is impossible or impractical to quantify the more central, substantive output of an organization, and when at the same time some exterior aspects of

9

the product, which are superficially related to its substance, are readily measurable. High schools which measure the quality of their curricula by the number of students who pass the Regents Examinations (stressing here one component of effectiveness) find that some teachers neglect the character-development of their students to drill them for the tests. If a pastor is frequently surveyed by his superiors as to how much money he has raised for a new cathedral or how many children attend Sunday school in his parish, he soon becomes more occupied with fund-raising and class size than with the spiritual guidance of his parishioners.

There is no complete solution to this problem. Organizations do best to recognize that many measures are far from accurate. Attributing too much importance to some indicators of organizational success and not enough to others may lead to considerable distortion of the organizational goals and undermine the very efficiency and effectiveness the organization seeks. Using measures of several aspects of the product (e.g., quantities and quality, as well as maintenance control), and stressing those features that come closest to the organizational goal reduces the problem of measuring organizational success, although one never succeeds in eliminating it.

The distortion of goals that arises from over-measurement of some aspects of the organizations's output to the detriment of others is one of a larger category of distortions that arise in the relations of organizations to their goals. In the following sections we are concerned with several other varieties of the distortion phenomenon. Distortions due to over-measurement are comparatively mild, since the main goals of the organization remain intact, though certain aspects of these goals become over-emphasized at the expense of other sometimes more important ones. Goals-displacement is much more detrimental.

Displacement of Goals

This severe type of organizational distortion was first explored 50 years ago by the German sociologist, Robert Michels. It arises when an organization displaces its goal—that is, substitutes for its legitimate goal some other goal for which it was not created, for which resources were not allocated to it, and which it is not known to serve.

The mildest and most common form of displacement is the process by which an organization reverses the priority between its goals and means in a way that makes the means a goal and the goals a means. The most common means so displaced is the organization itself. Organizations are instruments; they are created to serve one or more specific goals. But in the process of forming them, of granting them resources, and of recruiting personnel, interest groups are formed which are frequently concerned more with preserving and building up the organization itself than in helping it to serve its initial purpose. These interest groups use the organizational goals as means to recruit funds, to obtain tax exemptions or status in the community, in short, as means to their own goals.

Michels' book, *Political Parties*, is credited with the first extensive description and analysis of this not uncommon phenomenon of goal dis-

10

placement.[1] Michels studied the Socialist parties and labor unions in Europe before World War I. He pointed out that the parties and unions were formed to forward the Socialist revolution and to establish a democratic regime in authoritarian countries, such as Bismarck's Germany. In its efforts to serve these goals, the Socialist movement created party and union organizations. The organizations demanded leadership; the leaders soon developed vested interests in maintaining their positions, since loss of their organizational positions would have forced the leaders to return to manual labor, to a life of low prestige, low income, and without the psychological gratification of leadership. Michels showed that the leaders were, for these reasons, careful to establish themselves firmly in office. Through control over the means of communication of the organization and either the absorption into or "purging" from the organization of young, ambitious leaders, the established leaders strove to secure their positions. In this process, which Michels referred to as the "Iron Law of Oligarchy" (iron because it is presumably without exceptions, and oligarchy because the rule of a few is imposed), the organization's democratic goals, Michels maintains, were subverted. Furthermore, the leaders were less and less induced to take risks in their revolutionary activities for fear that they would anger the government, and so endanger the organization's existence. The party abandoned its militant activities in favor of increasing attention to development of a smoothly working organizational machine. More and more revolutionary moves were delayed to allow for "further preparations," which amounted to a large build-up of the organization, its assets, and the positions of the leaders. Thus, Michels suggested, organizations with revolutionary goals became quite conservative in their conduct.

Since Michels' statement of the Iron Law of Oligarchy this organizational tendency has been repeatedly documented. In many countries and in a variety of organizational types, even where the leadership is elected and can be changed by the membership, oligarchies prevail. Note, however, that Michels' study raises the question: Do limited-purpose organizations *need* to be democratic? Is this not a question of a misplaced concept, artificially transferred from the realm of public to that of private "government" in limited-purpose organizations? [2]

Michels and many of his followers seem not to have realized that an organization that is internally undemocratic might still serve the goal of forwarding the establishment of a democratic regime in the society in which it operates. It is even possible that an oligarchy by avoiding wasting efforts on internal strife, might direct the organizational membership more effectively in attaining democratic goals. It is however quite clear that even if there had been *no* displacement of the democratic goal in the organizations Michels studied, the goal of Socialist revolution was greatly diluted by persistent delays, and in all likelihood was eventually sacrificed in favor of preserving the organization.

Since Michels' work, goal displacement has been noted in a large

[1] Robert Michels, *Political Parties* (New York: Dover, 1959).
[2] See S. M. Lipset, M. A. Trow, and J. S. Coleman, *Union Democracy* (Glencoe, Ill.: The Free Press, 1956).

11

the organization goal: master or servant?

variety of organizations. S. D. Clark revealed it in his study of the Salvation Army in Canada.[3] He showed that as the organization grew larger and became more successful in its ability to obtain members and funds, the leadership began to devote more and more of its attentions and resources to the maintenance of the organization. It even gave up evangelical work in those parts of Canada where there was insufficient local financial support to maintain a chapter, presumably because such a chapter might become a drain on the organization's national resources.

Robert Merton discusses another major source of the same displacement tendency that Michels stressed.[4] Here goal displacement does not occur at the top of the organization but in its very body, and it occurs not in voluntary associations but in public and private bureaucracies. Merton suggested that bureaucracy has certain effects on its members' personalities, that it encourages the tendencies to adhere rigidly to rules and regulations for their own sake. We see that this may occur even when the organization formally or informally encourages flexibility in the application of the rules as part of its policy and as in line with its goals. For example, a welfare worker may fear the risks of making a decision on his own; he plays it safe by observing minutely the organization's rules and policies with the result that more important treatment considerations are underplayed. This is illustrated, for example, when a social worker in violation of his own judgment as to what would be most beneficial for the clients, recommends that a mentally disturbed child remain with his family, because the agency has a policy of not breaking up family units, even though the child's presence at home may disrupt the adjustment of the other children in the family. Instead of making procedures means to the organization's goal, he makes them ends in themselves. The policy becomes the prevailing criterion for decision, and the worker bends the clients' needs to fit the policy. Adherence to the organization's policy has become the organizational goal of the bureaucrat.

Another form which displacement can take was uncovered by Selznick when he depicted a situation known only too well to those who have ever worked for a governmental agency:

"Running an organization, as a specialized and essential activity, generates problems which have no necessary (and often opposed) relationship to the professed or 'original' goals of the organization. The day-to-day behavior of the group becomes centered around specific problems and approximate goals which have primarily an internal relevance. Then, since these activities come to consume an increasing proportion of the time and thoughts of the participants, they are—from the point of view of actual behavior—substituted for the professed goals."[5] The fixation on internal problems, which Selznick points out, operates to make the organization so turned in upon itself that it no longer serves its intended purpose.

[3] S. D. Clark, *Church and Sect in Canada* (Toronto: University of Toronto Press, 1948).

[4] Robert K. Merton, *Social Theory and Social Structure* (Glencoe, Ill.: The Free Press, 1957), pp. 197ff.

[5] Philip Selznick, "An Approach to a Theory of Bureaucracy," *American Sociological Review* (1943), 8:49. Quoted by David L. Sills in *The Volunteers* (Glencoe, Ill.: The Free Press, 1957), p. 64.

12

Goal Succession,
Multiplication, and Expansion

Similar in its sociological and psychological sources but quite different from the standpoint of meeting goals is the tendency of organizations to find new goals when the old ones have been realized or cannot be attained. A case in point is David Sills' *The Volunteers*,[6] a study of the Foundation for Infantile Paralysis, which is popularly known for its annual March of Dimes campaign. The major goal of the Foundation was to recruit public support for the medical research needed to fight polio and to provide assistance for its victims. As Sills reports, the Foundation was not diverted from its goal. On the contrary, in an effort that lasted two decades, it succeeded in providing many of the means that led to an almost complete elimination of polio; it supported much of the medical research done in this area which finally led to the famous Salk polio vaccine. The Foundation was then, so to speak, "unemployed." Here was a vast network of volunteers who experienced a variety of social and normative gratifications from working for the Foundation, and national leadership and staff, all coordinated in an efficient and obviously effective organizational machine —but the machine was without a purpose. The Foundation might simply have been disbanded, but instead the organization found a new goal—combating arthritis and birth defects. Sills' study illustrates both the deep vested interest that arises in maintaining the organization once it has been firmly established, and the service the goal performs for the organization (rather than the reverse). Without a goal, the Foundation's activity had no meaning for the members and no legitimacy in the community. It had to find a new goal or cease its activity.

Such clear-cut cases of goal-succession are rare both because most organizations do not reach their goals in any such definite way as the Polio Foundation did, and because many of those who do achieve their goals are dissolved as, for example, most anti-Nazi underground organizations were after the collapse of the Third Reich.

More common is the succession of goals when the service of the old one is highly unsuccessful, leaving the organization to find a new goal to serve if it is to survive. It is even more common for an organization in such a situation to set additional goals or expand the scope of their old ones. In doing this the organization acts to increase the dedication of its members and encourage the recruitment of new members. Thus undergraduate colleges in the United States over the last hundred years took on the goal of graduate training, a goal that is quite different from their original goal of producing gentlemen "who could read and write and stay out of jail." Many religious organizations added social and community service goals, which have, in some instances, superseded the older spiritual goals. Prayers are cut short, in some places, to leave more time for square dances. In another instance, the Red Cross, originally formed to "hold itself in readiness in the event of war or any calamity great enough to be considered

[6] Sills, *The Volunteers*, p. 64.

the organization goal: master or servant?

national, to inaugurate such practical measures in mitigation of the suffering and for the protection and relief of sick and wounded as may be consistent with the objects of the Association . . ." found itself underemployed after World War I and lost members, contributions, and public esteem.[7] It subsequently overcame that crisis by adding a goal—preserving and improving public health.

Thus the organization's self-interests may lead not only to displacement of primary goals by other secondary goals or by means, but also may lead the organization to actively seek new goals once the old ones are realized, or to acquire additional goals. Initially, these latter goals are often justified by the fact that they will enhance the service of the old goals, but often they become full-fledged equals if not "masters."

Multi-purpose Organizations

There are many organizations which simultaneously and legitimately serve two or more goals. Some add additional goals to original ones, but many organizations were originally formed to serve more than one goal at a time. In the field of scholarship there are more organizations which combine teaching with research (most universities) than there are organizations which are primarily devoted to teaching (most colleges), or which are devoted solely to research (e.g., the Rand Corporation; the Stanford Research Institute). While some hospitals are almost exclusively places where ill people are treated, many hospitals serve also as training grounds for the medical profession, and quite a few also are research centers. Most contemporary religious organizations combine a social with a spiritual goal.

To the extent that such things can be measured, it appears that many multi-purpose organizations tend to serve each of their goals separately and all of them together more effectively and efficiently than single-purpose organizations of the same category. For instance, many if not most high-quality hospitals serve three purposes—therapy, research, and teaching—while the hospitals which only cure, as most community hospitals do, are generally lower in the quality of medical care they offer.

Most of the important scientific discoveries of the past decade and most of the outstanding work in the social sciences stem from the faculties of universities where teaching and research are combined, not from the full-time personnel of research organizations. (Whether teaching is more effective in university colleges where research is emphasized or in colleges which devote themselves primarily to teaching is an open question. In part, the answer depends on the criteria of evaluation used, on whether or not one chooses to include character development in addition to acquiring knowledge and skills.) Finally, religious organizations serving middle-class areas in the contemporary United States could hardly fulfill their spiritual purposes without adding some social goals, because it is the social goals that attract many participants, at least initially, to dual-purpose churches. It seems that the community that stays together also prays together.

[7] Foster R. Dulles, *The American Red Cross: A History* (New York: Harper, 1950). Quoted by Sills, *op. cit.*, p. 262.

the organization goal: master or servant?

In part the relationship between effectiveness and multi-purpose organizations seems spurious—the result of extrinsic factors. For instance, multi-purpose organizations are more often found in the larger urban centers and single-purpose ones in smaller communities. Most major American universities and medical centers, for instance, are in, or close to, major cities. Since most professionals, when given a choice, prefer to live in urban centers, the multi-purpose organizations tend to have a larger pool of qualified professionals from which to recruit than single-purpose organizations. But the relationship between effectiveness and multi-purposeness seems to hold even if such extrinsic factors are held constant; for instance, if we compare single- and multi-purpose organizations in the same city—a college or research organization with a multi-purpose university in a major American city.

There are several internal reasons why multi-purpose organizations tend to be more effective than single-purpose ones. First of all, serving one goal often improves—within limits—the service rendered to another goal. For example, many researchers are stimulated by teaching intelligent, probing students. Researchers, in turn, bring new ideas to their teaching as well as a first-hand knowledge of the research experience in which they train their students. Second, as a rule multi-purpose organizations have greater recruitment appeal than single-purpose ones, in part because high quality is often associated with multi-services. It is difficult to think of many examples of mono-purpose organizations which have more prestige than their multi-purpose counterparts. Third, while some individuals prefer to deal exclusively in one service, many find combining two services more attractive because it allows them to gratify a wider variety of their personality needs. It also leaves more room for seasonal and life-cycle adjustment; e.g., stress on research in younger years and teaching in later ones, or the opposite.

There are, however, limits to the organization's ability to serve multi-purpose goals. Loss of effectiveness seems, for instance, to occur when all organizations of a specific category are made multi-purpose. In fields such as teaching or medicine, which have a cluster of associated activities, a large proportion of professionals prefer to participate in a combination of these activities. Some, however, devote their full attention to one or another and perform markedly better in one area than another. For this reason, effectiveness seems to be maximized when there are both single- and multi-purpose organizations in the profession, to allow both types of personalities to find employment most suited to their capacities and psychological needs.

Within multi-purpose organizations, certain types of conflict are unavoidable. The various goals often make incompatible demands on the organization. There may be conflicts over the amount of means, time, and energy to be allocated to each goal. For instance, the treatment goal of a hospital may be best served by a policy of open-admissions whereby anyone in need of hospitalization is accepted, while the research goal is best served by a policy of selective admissions which is concerned with providing sufficient numbers of specific types of illness as required by the staff's current research interests. The establishment of a set of priorities which clearly defines the relative importance of the various goals reduces the disruptive consequences of such conflicts, though it does not eliminate the problem.

Furthermore, serving a plurality of goals may create strains for personnel

For example, research demands specialization and allows the scholar to devote considerable time to investigate a particular, often seemingly minute, problem. Teaching, on the other hand, demands breadth of knowledge.

There is also the danger that one goal may completely subordinate the other and sometimes more primary one, such that the latter is no longer served effectively. A church may initiate social activities to attract members to religious services, but if the social activities consume the greater proportion of the church's resources or become the major focus of the participants' commitments, then they undermine the achievement of the religious goal. The statement, "The custom of the leading universities suggests that the equivalent of one day a week may be looked upon as a normal allotment of time for research," [8] is more an expression of concern over the dominating role this goal tends to acquire than an expression of a statistical norm. In short, multi-purpose organizations have their own major strains which derive in part from the very characteristics which make them, all things considered, more effective than single-purpose ones.

Goal Models and System Models

Thus far we have implicitly followed the widely held approach to organizational analysis that focuses on the study of goals and of organizations as their servants, obedient or otherwise. This approach has some distinct disadvantages both for studying and evaluating organizations. Those disadvantages are best brought into focus by comparing this more traditional approach with a newer one, which I advocate, and which will prevail, in much of the rest of this volume.

It is common for an outsider, if he is a researcher or evaluator (let us say a journalist or politician), to measure an organization against its goal or goals; the question most commonly asked about organizations is: How close did it come to achieving its assignment?

This approach has two potential pitfalls. First it tends, though not invariably, to give organizational studies a tone of social criticism rather than scientific analysis. Since most organizations most of the time do not attain their goals in any final sense, organizational monographs are frequently detoured into lengthy discussions about this lack of success to the exclusion of more penetrating types of analysis.[9] Low effectiveness is a general characteristic of organizations. Since goals, as symbolic units, are ideals which are more attractive than the reality which the organization attains, the organization can almost always be reported to be a failure. While this approach is valid, it is only valid from the particular viewpoint chosen by the researcher. This *goal-model* [10] approach defines success as a complete or at least a substantial realization of the organizational goal. Here the re-

---

[8] *The Faculty Handbook* of Columbia University, 1962, p. 31.

[9] For a discussion of this viewpoint and references to it in the literature, see Amitai Etzioni, "Two Approaches to Organizational Analysis: A Critique and a Suggestion," *Administrative Science Quarterly* (1960), 5:257–278.

[10] For a discussion of the concept model, see another book in this series, Alex Inkeles, *What is Sociology? An Introduction to the Discipline and Profession.* It is used here to refer to conceptual constructs, or meta-theories.

the organization goal: master or servant?

searcher is analogous to an electrical engineer who would rate all light bulbs "ineffective" since they convert only about 5 per cent of their electrical energy into light, the rest being "wasted" on heat. In practice, we find it more meaningful to compare light bulbs to one another rather than to some ideal "super bulb" that would turn all energy into light. It then becomes significant that brand "A" converts only 4.5 per cent of the energy into light while brand "B" converts 5.5 per cent. From the Olympian height of the goal—light without heat—both results are hopelessly inadequate. From the realistic level of comparative analysis, one bulb is 22 per cent more effective than the other (and may even be the most effective light bulb known).

Thus the goal-model approach is not the only means of evaluating organizational success. Rather than comparing existing organizations to ideals of what they might be, we may assess their performances relative to one another. We would not simply say that practically all organizations are oligarchic; we would rather try to determine which ones are more (or which are less) oligarchic than others. The comparative analysis of organizations suggests an alternative approach which we refer to as the *system model*. It constitutes a statement about relationships which must exist for an organization to operate.

Using a system model we are able to see a basic distortion in the analysis of organizations that is not visible or explicable from the perspective of goal-model evaluation. The latter approach expects organizational effectiveness to increase with the assignment of more means to the organization's goals. In the perspective of the goal model, to suggest that an organization can become more effective by assigning fewer means to goal activities is a contradiction. The system model, however, leads one to conclude that just as there may be too little allocation of resources to meet the goals of the organization, so there may also be an over-allocation of these resources. The system model explicitly recognizes that the organization solves certain problems other than those directly involved in the achievement of the goal, and that excessive concern with the latter may result in insufficient attention to other necessary organizational activities, and to a lack of coordination between the inflated goal activities and the de-emphasized non-goal activities. Thus a bank may pay all its attention to making money and completely ignore the morale of its employees. This lack of attention to non-goal activities may result in staff dissatisfaction which may express itself in poor work by the clerks which in turn results in decreased efficiency, or even in a wave of embezzlements which ultimately reduces the bank's effectiveness.

The system model is not free from drawbacks; it is more exacting and expensive when used for research. The goal model requires that the researcher determine the goals the organization is pursuing—and no more. If stated goals are chosen, this becomes comparatively easy. Real goals, those the organization actually pursues, are more difficult to establish. To find out the organization's real orientation, it is sometimes necessary not only to gain the confidence of its elite but also to analyze much of the organizational structure.

Research conducted on the basis of the system model requires more effort than a study following the goal model, even when the goal model focuses on real goals. The system model requires that the analyst determine what he considers a highly effective allocation of means. This often requires

17

considerable knowledge of the way an organization of the type studied functions. Acquiring such knowledge is often quite demanding, but (1) the efforts invested in obtaining the information required for the system model are not wasted, since the information collected in the process of developing the system model will be of much value for the study of most organizational problems; and (2) theoretical considerations may often serve as the bases for constructing a system model. This point requires some elaboration.

A well-developed organizational theory will include statements on the functional requirements [11] various organizational types must meet. Just as human beings have different needs, so organizations require different things to operate successfully. An awareness of these needs will guide the researcher who is constructing a system model for the study of a specific organization. In research where the pressure to economize is great, the theoretical system model of the particular organizational type may be used directly as a standard and guide for the analysis of a specific organization. But it should be pointed out that in the present state of organizational theory, such a model is often not available. At present, organizational theory is generally constructed on a high level of abstraction, dealing mainly with general propositions which apply equally well—but also equally badly—to all organizations. The differences among various organizational types are considerable; therefore any theory of organizations in general must be highly abstract. It can serve as an important frame for specification—that is, for the development of special theoretical models for the various organizational types—but it cannot substitute for such theories by serving in itself as a system model, to be applied directly to the analysis of actual organizations.[12]

Maybe the best support for the thesis that a system model can be formulated and fruitfully applied is found in a study of organizational effectiveness by B. S. Georgopoulos and A. S. Tannenbaum,[13] one of the few studies that distinguish explicitly between the goal and system approaches to the study of effectiveness. Instead of focusing on the goals of the delivery service organizations under study, the researchers constructed three indexes, each measuring one basic element of the system. These were: (1) station productivity, (2) intraorganizational strain as indicated by the incidence of tension and conflict among organizational subgroups, and (3) organizational flexibility, defined as the ability to adjust to external or internal change. The total score of effectiveness thus produced was significantly correlated with the ratings on effectiveness which various experts and "insiders" gave the 32 stations. The stations were compared to one another on these dimensions rather than to an idealized picture of what a delivery station should be.

Further development of such system-effectiveness indexes will require elaboration of organizational theory along the lines discussed above, because

[11] Functional requirements, here and throughout this volume, simply refer to the requirements that have to be met for the specific unit under discussion to function—that is, to operate. For a more extensive discussion of this important concept, see Inkeles *What is Sociology?*

[12] For an effort to provide models for the analysis of various types of organizations, see Amitai Etzioni, *A Comparative Analysis of Complex Organizations* (New York: The Free Press of Glencoe, 1961).

[13] B. S. Georgopoulos and A. S. Tannenbaum, "A Study of Organizational Effectiveness," *American Sociological Review* (1957), 22:534–540.

the organization goal: master or servant?

it is necessary to supply a rationale for measuring certain aspects of the system and not others.

Survival and Effectiveness Models

A system model constitutes a statement about relationships which, if actually existing, would allow an organization to maintain itself and to operate. There are two major sub-types of system models. One may be called a survival model—i.e., a set of requirements which, if fulfilled, allows the system to exist. In such a model, each relationship specified is a prerequisite for the functioning of the system; remove any one of them and the system ceases to operate, like an engine whose sparkplugs have been removed. The second sub-type is an effectiveness model. It defines a pattern of interrelations among the elements of the system which would make it most effective in the service of a given goal, as compared to other combinations of the same or similar elements. The question here is: Which type of sparkplug makes the engine run smoothest?

There is considerable difference between the two sub-models. Alternatives which are equally satisfactory from the viewpoint of the survival model have a different value from the viewpoint of the effectiveness model. The survival model gives a "yes" or "no" score when answering the question: Is a specific relationship necessary? The effectiveness model tells us the relative effectiveness of several alternatives; there are first, second, third, and n'th choices. Only rarely are two patterns full-fledged alternatives in this sense— i.e., only rarely do they have the same effectiveness value. The survival model would not record significant changes in organizational operations; the model only asks whether the basic requirements of the organization are being met. The use of the effectiveness model evaluates changes that have occurred in the organization, and how they affect the ability of the organization to serve its goals, as compared to its earlier state or other organizations of its kind.

the classical
approach

three

The search for greater effectiveness and efficiency in organizations gave rise to the *Classical Theory* of Administration, perhaps more appropriately called *Scientific Management*, since this latter title expresses the emphasis of this organizational approach: Workers were seen as motivated by economic rewards, and the organization was characterized by a clearly defined division of labor with a highly specialized personnel and by a distinct hierarchy of authority. Out of this tradition comes the characterization of the *formal organization* as a blueprint according to which organizations are to be constructed and to which they ought to adhere.

Arising in part as a reaction to Scientific Management, another school of thinking gained prominence in the United States—*Human Relations*. In contrast to Classical Theory, Human Relations emphasized the emotional, unplanned, non-rational elements in organizational behavior. It discovered the significance of friendship and social groupings of workers for the organization. It also pointed out the importance of leadership in the organization and of emotional communication and participation. From these observations the concept of *informal organization* was developed. This is sometimes viewed as what there is to organization beyond the formal structure; sometimes, as what the organizational life is really like, as distinct from blueprint and charts.

It remained the task of a third tradition in organizational thinking to relate the two concepts of the formal and informal organization and to provide a more complete and integrated picture of the organization. This great con-

20

vergence of organizational theory, the *Structuralist approach,* was made considerably more sophisticated through comparative analysis. Whereas the earlier schools focused their attention largely on factories and to some degree on public administration, and were only later adapted to the study of other organizations, the scope of the structuralist approach was much broader to begin with, both in terms of the kinds of organizations covered and the kinds of cultural background taken into account.

Not only do these three schools differ in their views of the organization, but they suggest quite different conceptions of man and society. While none of the three approaches is exclusively concerned with serving either the organizational goals as viewed by management or the workers' goals, there are important differences as to the goals emphasized in each of the different approaches. The Classical approach recognized no conflict between man and organization. It viewed the organization from a highly managerial standpoint. It assumed that what was good for management was good for the workers. The Classical School argued that hard and efficient labor will in the end pay off for both groups by increasing the effectiveness of the organization: Higher productivity leads to higher profits which in turn lead to higher pay and greater worker satisfaction.

The Human Relations School pointed out that the workers have many needs other than purely economic ones, and that the Classical approach benefits neither management nor the workers. They went on to suggest ways in which management could—by paying attention to the non-economic, social and cultural needs of the workers—increase worker satisfaction *and* productivity. The Structuralist School, we shall see, views some conflict and strain between man and organization as inevitable and by no means always undesirable.

The Classical
Motivational Theory

The Classical approach contained both a theory of motivation and one of organization. The central contribution to the motivational theory was made by Frederick W. Taylor [1] in what became known as Scientific Management. Scientific Management combines a study of physical capabilities of a worker, as is still done (primarily by engineers) in time and motion studies, with an economic approach which views man as driven by the fear of hunger and the search for profit. The central tenet of the approach is that if material rewards are closely related to work efforts, the worker will respond with the maximum performance he is physically capable of.

Although Taylor originally set out to study the interaction between human characteristics and the characteristics of the machine, the relationship between those two elements which make up the industrial work process, he ended up by focusing on a far more limited subject: the physical characteristics of the human body in routine jobs—e.g., shoveling coal or picking up loads. Eventually Taylor came to view human and machine resources not so much as mutually adaptable, but rather man functioning as an appendage to the industrial machine.

[1] Frederick W. Taylor, *Scientific Management* (New York: Harper, 1911).

Taylor's students, the human engineers, searched for the physical limits of human performance, put in terms of loads, pace, and fatigue. For example, they studied how many hours and at what speed a worker could carry loads of 50 pounds. Fatigue was viewed exclusively as a muscular, physiological phenomenon. Efforts were made to find motions that were less fatiguing and hence allowed the same human body to carry out more work with the same degree of fatigue in a given time unit. The following are some typical propositions of Scientific Management:

1. The two hands should begin and complete their motions simultaneously.

2. Smooth, continuous motions of the hands are preferable to zig-zag or straight-line motions involving sudden and sharp changes in direction.

3. Proper illumination increases productivity.

4. There should be a definite and fixed place for all the tools and materials.

Payment, it was suggested, should be made to the worker in closest possible association with output. Various methods of measuring worker output and ways of relating payment to it were devised. Many of these methods are highly complicated, and of interest mainly to specialists; the principles of the system remain simple, however: (1) pay should be on merit of performance and no other criterion (e.g., seniority); (2) the time unit should be as small as possible; monthly salaries are highly undesirable; wages paid by the hour are better; but the ideal situation is piece-work wages in which pay is directly dependent on the actual amount of work accomplished.

Taylor and his associates had little doubt that once the best working procedure was taught to a worker (use both hands, etc.) and his pay was tied to his output, he could be induced to produce the maximum physically possible as calculated by the time and motion engineers.

The Classical
Organizational Theory

Adam Smith's description of modern manufacturing of pins, in his *The Wealth of Nations*, has become a classic illustration of the significance of division of labor. This illustration also illustrates a basic principle of the school of Scientific Management. Smith notes that a worker by himself might produce 20 pins a day. But by breaking down the task of making pins into many simple operations (he estimated that there were about 18 different jobs, such as straightening the wire and cutting it) Smith stated that he had seen ten workers produce 48,000 pins in a day. This represents 4,800 pins per worker, or 240 times what he could produce alone. The division of labor that Smith first noted in 1776 was to become the basis of a theory of organizational efficiency over a hundred years later.

The Classical administration theory, presented in works by Gulick and Urwick,[2] made the division of labor its central tenet. The Classical approach rests firmly on the assumption that the more a particular job can

[2] Luther Gulick and L. Urwick (eds.), *Papers on the Science of Administration* (New York: Institute of Public Administration, Columbia University, 1937).

the classical approach

be broken down into its simplest component parts, the more specialized and consequently the more skilled a worker can become in carrying out his part of the job. The more skilled the worker becomes in fulfilling his particular job, the more efficient the whole production system will be.

The *division* of labor, the Classical approach pointed out, has to be balanced by a *unity* of control. The tasks have to be broken up into components by a central authority in line with a central plan of action; the efforts of each work unit need to be supervised; and the various job efforts leading to the final product have to be coordinated. Since each supervisor has a limited number of subordinates he can effectively control, it is necessary to appoint a number of first-line supervisors, and following that, a second-line supervisor (to supervise the supervisors), and so on up. Each 5 to 6 workers, for instance, need one first-line supervisor; every 6 first-line supervisors, and hence, every 40 workers, need 1 second-line supervisor, and so on. The number of subordinates controlled by one superior defines his "span or control." What results is a *pyramid of control* leading up to one top executive. In this way, the whole organization can be controlled from one *center of authority*, without having any one supervisor control more than 5 to 10 subordinates.

While all the classical writers accepted the principles of need for supervision and a single center of authority and control in the organization, they differed on how these principles should be implemented. The disagreement centered on the most efficient way the work should be distributed among the elementary production units and how the organizational pyramid of control should be constructed. Most Classical writers, however, agreed that work in the organization should be specialized according to 1 or more of 4 basic principles. By following these principles, the organization could achieve the optimal division of labor and authority.

The first principle stated that specialization should be by *purpose* of the task. Workers who serve similar goals or sub-goals in the organization should be attached to the same organizational division. There would be as many divisions in the organization as there are goals or sub-goals. The United States armed forces, for instance, share the general goal of protecting the country. But parts of the armed forces have different sub-goals: The navy is responsible for defense on the seas; the air force must guard against attack from the air; and the army is responsible for land defense.

The second principle of specialization suggests that all work based on a particular *process* should be grouped together, since it must share a special fund of knowledge and requires the use of similar skills or procedures. For example, the 3 military branches all need intelligence information. The Central Intelligence Agency provides certain kinds of intelligence information that are used by all 3 branches, an example of an organization divided according to process.

Specialization according to type of *clientele* is still another basis for division. All work directed to serve a specific group of clients is placed in one division. For example, teachers who instruct very young children are separated from teachers who instruct adolescents.

The fourth principle says that jobs performed in the same *geographical area* should be placed together. Here different types of jobs may fall in the same division as long as they are carried out in the same place. According to

23

this principle, all the United States military units (Navy, Air Force, and Army) in Southeast Asia are under one command.

This four-principle approach has been severely criticized. The principles are difficult to apply to a specific organization since they often overlap, are sometimes incompatible with one another, and are quite vague. Take, for example, building missiles for military use. Should the missile program be assigned to one branch of the armed forces or all three, since missiles can be used on land, sea, and air? Should we have a single missile force because all missile-building requires a common fund of knowledge? Should we build a number of different regional forces because some missiles are built for Europe's defense and some for U.S. defense? It is difficult not to conclude that the 4 principles fail to provide a satisfactory guide to division of labor in the organization.

Furthermore it has been pointed out that these principles are prescriptive rather than descriptive, that they state how work should be divided rather than how work actually is divided. The actual planning of the division of labor in a given organization is affected by many considerations not covered by the 4 principles. The type of specialization may be determined by the culture in which the organization is situated (e.g., labor unions in Russia *vs.* those in the U.S.A.); by the environment of the organization (e.g., ecology which makes for easy *vs.* difficult communication); the availability and type of personnel (e.g., high unemployment *vs.* scarcity of labor); and by political factors (e.g., which division of labor will be less acceptable and which more acceptable to the labor union). Moreover, organizations are often not planned ahead of time in such great detail, and when they are, the plans are often dispensed with or largely modified because of considerations other than the 4 principles. Organizations grow, develop, divide, and merge in patterns that are only partially predictable and under the control of management. Designing an organization is somewhat like planning a forest, and generally not like designing a building. In short, the 4 traditional principles for dividing labor in the organization neither allow for a realistic analysis of existing organizations nor do they in fact provide workable plans for improvement. "Even if a decision is made to follow, say, a product/purpose/pattern, there will remain numerous questions of just what activities belong in each division. For example, a retail store is a product pattern, but this still leaves unanswered the question of whether each department is free to do its own credit work, whether delivery will be centralized, what kind of accounting records should be maintained and who will keep them, and so forth." [3]

In reality, organizations are made up of a combination of various layers that differ in their degree of specialization. The tendency is often for the lower layers to be organized according to area and/or clientele principles, and the higher ones by purpose and/or process. But even this statement should be viewed only as a probability statement which says that effective organizations are *likely* to be this way, rather than saying that they always or even usually are. Many of the problems which we deal with in the following chapters arise from the fact that in actuality organizations often combine

[3] William H. Newman, *Administrative Action* (Englewood Cliffs, N.J.: Prentice-Hall, 1950), p. 128.

the classical approach

work units and divisions whose organizational principles are only partially compatible. We will see that it is not only possible to find contradictory principles operating simultaneously in the same organization, but that such "mix" provides the most effective organization.

The application of the Classical approach with its concern for formal organizational structure has by no means died out. Some continue to apply it as if it had never been criticized. Some new and fruitful developments, however, have arisen out of the Classical tradition, especially efforts to find an empirical basis for studying administration.[4] The major modification of the Classical approach has been the tendency away from prescribing the "right" organizational structure to exploring why certain forms of organizational structure are more effective than others. This is best seen in the Neo-Classical approach found in a volume by Simon, Smithburg, and Thompson.[5] The approach is Classical in that it still pays considerable attention to formal structure and to rational considerations; it differs from the traditional approach in studying the actual ways values (or goals and subgoals) of an organization can be and are implemented. The values discussed by Simon, Smithburg, and Thompson are: accountability, expertness and economy, level of conflict settlement, policy development, and program emphasis.

Accountability

Only the naive, inexperienced administrator would assume that orders properly issued will as a rule be properly carried out. Therefore there is a constant need to provide mechanisms of control to check on fulfillment of orders and adherence to regulation from quality specification to safety rules. Largely this task of supervision is built into the hierarchy of authority, i.e., the role of "higher-in-rank" includes the obligation to check on the performance of the lower-in-rank. However, to the degree that such enforcement through organizational hierarchy is not sufficient, specialized control agencies tend to develop; these are units outside the regular line structure (see below) which are in charge of enforcing specific sets of rules or orders (e.g., level of quality). In this sense, their enforcement mandate differs from that of the line which is generally diffuse. An example of such a specialized unit is the comptroller department which acts as an agency especially concerned with costs, efficiency, and financial records. Adding such special control units to regular line control increases the accountability of an organization. This is an approach that draws on organizational reality and helps to improve it; on paper, regular line control can seem to be quite sufficient.

Accountability is likely to increase efficiency, but it also often produces tensions, as shown by the following report of a foreman of a finishing department:

> Once we had a job putting a baked enamel finish on some metal panels about five feet long and a foot wide. We would spray the enamel on one

[4] See J. G. March and H. Simon, *Organizations* (New York: Wiley, 1958).
[5] H. A. Simon, D. W. Smithburg, and V. A. Thompson, *Public Administration* (New York: Knopf, 1959).

25

side, rack them up flat on a truck, and shove the truck into the baking oven. When they would come out, this inspector would tilt each one up to the light, and if he would see even one dust speck, he would send it back; said the specifications called for perfectly smooth finish. Well our spray room and oven weren't in too good shape and it was almost impossible to get one completely dust free. It was crazy to be so strict; it was only a protective enamel for an inside surface that was never seen, but this guy didn't care. Finally we got the engineers to look at the job and they told him it was good enough the way we were doing it.

Thus organizations tend both to limit special enforcement agencies, to refrain from building up tensions to an explosive point, and to provide means for "appeals," to counter excessively zealous accountants and supervisors.[6]

Expertness and Economy

While some specialized units are in charge of "extra" enforcement, a far greater number of them are mainly concerned with carrying out specific sets of activities as a service for the main production units. Statistical analysis, computer services, traffic, legal advice, printing, and stenographic pools are typical examples of such units.

Here the central question for organizational specialization has shifted away from the earlier question: Should the principle of "purpose" or "process" determine which is the most efficient organization? to the question: What is the best way to combine multi-functional units (or "purpose" units) with single-functional specialized units (or "process" units)? since most organizations utilize both kinds. A typical case in point is the articulation of the work of the planning staff with that of the production units.

It is generally agreed that the less the need for a certain kind of activity —let us say electronic data processing—in a multi-functional unit like a university department, the greater the economy that can be attained by concentrating all such activities on behalf of the various multi-functional units into one single-functional unit. This will permit the use of full-time personnel in the jobs, allowing the employees to become experts, or for the unit to hire experts. It also allows for greater routinization of the job. On the other hand, such concentration will often involve some loss of knowledge of the particular needs of the various multi-functional units which use the "same" services. For instance, the programers of the central computer service are likely to be unfamiliar with the technical terms and symbols used by various departments. In addition there are likely to be communication and transportation costs which may well offset, if not outweigh, the gains due to concentration by function. This is especially apparent when by increasing the efficiency of low-salaried personnel, one reduces the efficiency of high-salaried ones: e.g., by concentrating the work in a pool, 4 typists may do the work of 5, but the executive time spent in coordinating may be more expensive than the cost of an extra typist. Moreover, a major source of motivation for efficient work might lie in the attachment to a multi-functional unit; typists,

[6] Quoted in B. B. Gardner and D. G. Moore, *Human Relations in Industry* (Homewood, Ill.: Irwin, 1952), p. 77.

26

the classical approach

as a rule, prefer to work for a particular boss or department rather than in a pool. There is no hard and fast rule for determining the best balance between these two types of division of labor. It varies greatly with the kind of tasks that are involved in the output of the organization. Generally, however, the less-skilled the jobs, the less the need for a concentration in single-functional units.

Levels-of-Conflict Settlement

The functions of a control pyramid are not only to supervise, coordinate, and check on performances, but also to provide points at which conflicts can be resolved. Supervisors, organizational units, or staff divisions often come into conflict with one another either because the principles that divide the labor among them and prescribe their relations are not clear, or because the prescribed rules are being adhered to by some but not by others, or because differences of interest, viewpoint, or personalities need to be reconciled. Such conflicts, especially if they are allowed to simmer, may sharply reduce the efficiency of the organization. Providing for any two employees and for any two organizational units, one point of authority to which both are subordinate and at which conflicts can be settled is viewed as essential to organizational efficiency.

Simon, Smithburg, and Thompson point to several advantages of resolving conflict at relatively low levels in the organizational hierarchy. Low-level settlement reduces the work load of the most burdened and most "expensive" higher-level executives. It permits rapid settlement of disagreements since the lines of communication are shorter, and it permits the executive who must serve as judge or arbiter to have a relatively full command of the facts and to be able to draw on his personal knowledge of the conflicting parties.

At the same time, it is widely recognized that conflict is not necessarily a bad thing, nor a thing to be hidden from higher ranks. Conflict might involve organization-wide or "high policy" matters, and in this case it would be better to take the conflict as far up in the hierarchy as necessary to obtain a modification or re-affirmation of policy rather than find a way around the problem—a typical lower-level "solution." Furthermore, face-to-face relations can make conflict settlement more, rather than less, difficult. The more personal contact the arbitrator of a dispute has had with the conflicting parties, the more disruptive the settlement of that dispute is likely to be for his relationship with one or both of the opposing sides. Having an employee's supervisor or foreman side with his opponent can hardly improve that employee's relationship to his supervisor. Ultimately, the questions as to whether high- or low-level conflict settlement is more desirable, and under what conditions one is better than the other, are matters for empirical research.

Program Emphasis

To counter the tendency (discussed earlier) for the organization to replace its initial goals with what were formerly its means, the founders of the organization may take certain protective measures when designing and establishing the organization. By patterning the organization in such a way that it will emphasize direct service of its goal over service of

27

its means, and by structuring its division of labor and hierarchy of authority accordingly, the founders can lessen the probability that the organization will grow to deviate from its original purposes. More power may be given those in command of direct services to goals than those who deal with more removed matters; for instance, certain personnel may be permitted easier access to top executives. Means activities might be distributed among various units that service the goals directly. This assures that the executives in charge of the goal activities also control the means activities. Thus, faculty committees may be assigned the job of supervising expansion plans of a university in order to make sure that these plans will be consistent with the primary educational goals of the organization rather than oriented to the convenience of the builder. The physical location of divisions in the organization may also strengthen the priority of goals over means. The effect of locating some civilian advisers on military affairs in the White House vs. locating them in the Pentagon illustrates this point.

Centralization vs. Decentralization

No less important than many of the features examined by Simon, Smithburg, and Thompson is the question of the effect of centralization on the efficiency and effectiveness of an organization. In terms of the Classical approach, the question is: Whenever there are two or more organizational units, with one (or more) of them superior to the others in decision-making authority, which decisions should be left to the lower one(s), and which should be made by the higher unit(s)? The more decision-making authority held by those lower in the authority structure (and larger in number), the less centralized the organization is.

Low centralization may be achieved either by limiting the *kinds* of decisions that have to be referred upward or at least approved at a higher level (e.g., "you have to check on the price of material that you intend to order but you are free to decide on the quantities you need"), or by increasing the *degree* of autonomy given to the unit in each issue (e.g., "you don't have to check with superiors on purchases involving less than a thousand dollars"). Many factors affect the level of centralization: the cultural norms (centralization is more "acceptable" to the Germans than the British), educational level of the unit heads (the higher the level of education, the greater the decentralization the organization can tolerate), the personality of the top executive, and so on. Students of formal organization have been more interested in the effect on the organization of such factors as the amount and type of coordination between units—e.g., is there a regular meeting of department heads?

In addition, the availability of specialized service units is known to affect the amount of centralization in the organization since these units are usually too specialized and costly to be attached to the lower levels of the organization. Instituting a computer section in a large organization often increases centralization because it becomes necessary to have a highly coordinated schedule to allow all departments to use the computer. This necessitates increased communication between departments and often results in more centralized planning and control throughout the organization.

28

**School Practices in 16 Independent
and 16 Centrally Controlled School Systems**

School Practices	Independent Schools	Centrally Controlled Schools
Movable classroom furniture used	11	0
Teacher experimentation encouraged by superintendency	12	6
Course of study developed cooperatively by local teachers	14	2
Adequate provision for vocational education	6	16
Provision for pupils with special disabilities	8	16
Adequate tenure provisions	2	16
Total schools studied	16	16

Allen H. Barton, *Organizational Measurement and Its Bearing on The Study of College Environments* (Princeton: College Entrance Examination Board, 1961), p. 26.

The preceding evidence supports our intuition that centralized organizations allow for less local experimentation and grant less unit-flexibility, although they are more likely to be able to provide facilities that independent units could not afford, and to enforce "labor relations" standards, such as tenure, more efficiently.

Nor is de-centralization always welcome—at least initially. For example:

One company made a change in its accounting organization which broke up large accounting units in a central location into small units in shop location. This removed the members of the organization from the preferred office location and put them in the lower-status shop environment. It also separated them into small groups isolated from each other, and broke up many of their cliques and social activities which they had carried on as one large group. Furthermore, they were in much less frequent contact with their superiors and felt that they were isolated and ignored. The adjustment to this change required several months, during which time there were continual complaints about the change, about the poor working conditions, the noise and dirt in the new location, the isolation from higher supervisors, anxieties about being lost in the shop, and many similar expressions of disturbance.[7]

Decision-making Theory

An important though relatively new and less developed addition to the formal line of organizational analysis is the study of organizational decision-making. The theory of decision-making is at present

[7] *Ibid.*, p. 301.

largely a non-organizational theory that deals with decisions made by individuals, disregarding whether the individuals are card players, shoppers in a supermarket, or executives. Moreover, like the Classical administrative approach, decision-making theory in large part is prescriptive; i.e., it indicates—often on the basis of mathematical analysis and logical reasoning, sometimes on the basis of "distilled common sense"—what steps a decision-maker *should* follow if he wishes to make a rational decision. However, in recent years there has been growing interest in a descriptive theory of decision-making which reports and analyzes how people actually make decisions, what prevents them from making rational ones, and under what conditions they will make comparatively rational decisions. The descriptive approach still requires considerable development and needs to be extended from the individual to the organization level.

In a book that opened a whole new vista of administration theory, Herbert A. Simon pointed out that organizations are based on not one but two modes of division of labor and specialization.[8] In addition to the recognized type of horizontal specialization—division of labor according to a particular task—there is a vertical specialization. Here division of labor is based on power rather than work; jobs are more or less performance-jobs or decision-making ones. Simon pointed out that the higher the rank, the more jobs consist of decision-making, and fewer actual performances are carried out. In a typical factory, the job of the worker is almost all performance; the supervisor's job contains some performance and some decision-making duties; and the higher-level administrator spends nearly all his time making decisions; —that is, telling lower-in-ranks what to tell their subordinates to do.

Decision-making itself is divided in a way that makes the higher-in-rank set the wider policy lines while the lower-echelon administrators break the policy down into more detailed decisions. In this way the whole organization can be viewed as an efficient tool, with general policy-making concentrated at the top, policy specification carried out by the middle ranks, and actual work performance carried out by the lower ranks. This division of policy-making and performance is a common (but by no means the only) mode of efficient allocation of decision-making and work.[9] In hospitals, for instance, both the most crucial decisions *and* the most crucial performances are carried out by the same personnel; namely, the highly trained physicians. We shall return to this point below when professional organizations are discussed.

March and Simon made a most important addition to this conception of organizational decision-making in their examination of search behavior.[10] The question they posited was: Under what conditions does an organization attempt to change its behavior by searching for more rational modes of serving its goal(s)? The general line of thought that was previously held, at least implicitly (especially in the writings of the Classical school), was that organizations endlessly search for the optimum rational behavior—i.e., the best possible pattern of organization—and will rest only when that is attained. March and Simon suggest that organizations seek a *satisfying* solu-

[8] H. A. Simon, *Administrative Behavior* (New York: Macmillan, 1945).

[9] Amitai Etzioni, "Authority Structure and Organizational Effectiveness," *Administrative Science Quarterly* (1959), 4:43–67.

[10] March and Simon, *Organizations, op. cit.*

30

the classical approach

tion rather than an optimum one. This means that search behavior will be stopped once a pattern is found which is considered "reasonably good," "acceptable." A new search will be triggered when organizational performance falls below that level.

There is one type of organizational sub-unit that is a partial exception to the March and Simon hypothesis. The research and development divisions in organizations are deliberately constructed to enable the organization to continue search activity even when most of the organization's members are quite satisfied. The satisfaction of this division depends both on its success in finding and developing innovation and in gaining acceptance for these innovations by the organization. Research and development units neither move the organization to function at its optimal capacity nor do they rest when it does "reasonably well." Rather they tend to define for the organization successively higher levels of satisfaction, by raising the standards of what is considered "all right." In this way organizations have been able to build in mechanisms to make themselves "rationally dissatisfied" and continue in search of improvement.

It is a long way from the studies of coal-shoveling and fatigue to the sophisticated analysis of March and Simon; however, the major focus of their approach remains basically the formal organization,[11] rational behavior, the search for the organizational tool most suited to serve a given set of goals, and not the organizational tool that keeps its participants most happy. The central questions are how is an organization best patterned, in terms of division of labor and of authority, and which patterns of coordination are the most effective; the stress is on choices individuals make for the organization (and its units) rather than on the factors that limit their choices or bias their decisions. In the following chapter our focus shifts to many of the factors this approach largely neglected. This neglect, however, should not mislead us. A full half of what organizational analysis is all about—namely, the formal organization—is covered by the Classical and Neo-Classical approach.

[11] Technically defined, *formal organization* is the pattern of division of tasks and power among the organizational position, and the rules expected to guide the behavior of the participants, as defined by management.

from

human relations

to the

structuralists

four

The Human Relations approach was born out of a reaction to the Classical formal approach. It focused on elements in the organization which were of small or no concern to the Classical approach. Elton Mayo is generally recognized as the father of the school; John Dewey indirectly and Kurt Lewin most directly also contributed much to its initiation. Mayo and his associates discovered that: (1) the amount of work carried out by a worker (and hence the organizational level of efficiency and rationality) is not determined by his physical capacity but by his social "capacity"; (2) non-economic rewards play a central role in determining the motivation and happiness of the worker; (3) the highest specialization is by no means the most efficient form of division of labor; and (4) workers do not react to management and its norms and rewards as individuals but as members of groups. Above all, the Human Relations School, for reasons which we shall soon discuss, emphasized the role of communication, participation, and leadership. Each of these insights was documented by one or more experiments or field studies, many of which have become "classics," widely referred to by social scientists.

Physical vs. Social Determinants of Output

The first of these studies was conducted at the Western Electric Company's Hawthorne Works in Chicago from 1927 to 1932; this series of studies (of which we discuss only a part) have come to

32

be known as the Hawthorne studies. From the first, there were some highly unexpected findings. Roethlisberger and Dickson in their volume, *Management and the Worker*,[1] point out that in testing the effect of increased illumination on the level of production (the theories of Scientific Management predicted that better illumination would result in increased productivity), the investigators were amazed to find that no relation existed between these two variables. In fact, in one of the later studies where workers were placed in a control room, the results indicated that productivity continued to increase even when illumination was decreased! It only dropped off after the light became so dim that workers could not see properly.

This puzzling finding sparked a series of studies which, one by one, brought into question statements of Classical writers that there was a simple and direct relationship between physical working conditions and rate of production. Following the research on illumination, the investigators tested the effect of rest breaks on the production of 5 workers placed in a test room. A number of different combinations of 5-, 10-, and 15-minute rest periods were tried out to judge their differential effect on production rates. While the rate of production showed a fairly consistent and general increase, it was not related to increases in the rest breaks and hence could not be attributed to them. This fact was surprisingly demonstrated when after the rest breaks were abolished at the end of the experiment, and the longer "fatiguing" work day was restored, production continued higher in the experimental group than the general factory rate.[2] The conclusion was that there was, ". . . no evidence in support of the hypothesis that the increased output rate . . . was due to relief from fatigue." A suggestion about what factors were accountable for the increased production as well as for the general improvement in the attitude of the workers came from the investigators in the form of a hypothesis: Increased production was the result of the changed social situation of the workers, modifications in their level of psychological satisfaction, and new patterns of social interaction, brought about by putting them into the experiment room and the special attention involved. The discovery of the significance of "social factors" was to become the major finding of the Hawthorne studies.

The crucial breakthrough in research came with the famous Bank Wiring Room experiment involving the wiring of switchboards. This experiment called into question virtually all the assumptions of Scientific Management. Many additional studies have since elaborated and verified the findings of the Bank Wiring Study. When this experiment was set up, the researchers were already aware that worker groups made ineffectual the individual and group piecework pay system which management had set up. The workers were producing far less than they were physically capable of; they were following a social norm enforced by their co-workers, which defined the proper amount of production, rather than trying to fill the quota management engineers thought they could achieve, even though this quota allowed them to earn as much as they physically could. The phrase "artificial restriction of output" was coined by the observers of this phenomenon, to contrast it with the "natural" output that was physically possible.

[1] F. J. Roethlisberger and W. J. Dickson, *Management and the Worker* (Cambridge: Harvard University Press, 1939).
[2] *Ibid.*, p. 127.

33

What actually happened in the group that resulted in self-imposed quota restrictions? A group of 14 workers was set up as a work unit in a separate room in which they were closely observed for 6 months. Their job was to wire telephone switchboards (called "banks") which required some individual work and some group cooperation. The payment system used was similar to that of the rest of the company. The workers were paid individual hourly rates, based on their individual average output, plus a bonus that was determined by the average group output. In addition, they were given individual allowances for work stoppages beyond their control so that more efficient producers would not be penalized by work lags caused by the less efficient workers. In line with Taylor's theories on incentives, the managerial assumptions were that the men would work as hard as they could, since the harder they worked the more hourly pay they would receive; that they would strive to cooperate and coordinate their efforts, since this would further increase their income by increasing group productivity; and that detailed and accurate records would be available both on output and causes of stoppage which would serve to set the amount of pay of the workers.

In practice, the men set a norm of the "proper day's work," which was for each man to wire two complete sets of equipment each day. Workers who produced more were ridiculed as "speed kings" and criticized as "rate busters." Those who worked considerably less were labeled "chiselers." The actual production averages were, over the months, day in and day out, surprisingly close to the group's norms. There was much pressure not to reveal to the foreman and other management personnel that the workers could produce much more. The workers firmly believed that if they produced a great deal more, their pay rate would be reduced or some of them would lose their jobs (the study took place during the Great Depression), and that if they produced considerably less, they would be unfair to management ("not provide a day's work for a day's pay") and this would also "get them into trouble." Neither belief had any basis in the practices of the company under study. Management was not much more realistic; it thought that 2 boards a day was about all a hard working man *could* wire.

Following are the major findings and conclusions of the Hawthorne experiments:

1. *The level of production is set by social norms, not by physiological capacities*, a point already illustrated by earlier studies of illumination and fatigue.

2. *Non-economic rewards and sanctions significantly affect the behavior of the workers and largely limit the effect of economic incentive plans.* Two rewards and sanctions were particularly powerful and both were "symbolic" rather than material. Workers who produced significantly more (or less) than the socially determined norm lost the *affection* and *respect* of their co-workers and friends. All the workers in the wiring room clearly preferred maintaining amicable relations with their friends to making more money. In a later study, Melville Dalton showed that this is not always the case.[3] He found that those who were "rate busters" were individuals whose education and social ex-

---

[3] This study is reported in William F. Whyte, *et al.*, *Money and Motivation* (New York: Harper, 1955), pp. 39–49.

from human relations to the structuralists

perience taught them how to get along with less affection and respect, at least in the work context. Dalton found that none of the 98 practicing Catholics in the groups he studied was a rate buster and that only one of the eight rate busters was born a Catholic. (Catholics are believed to be more "sociable" and sensitive to affection and respect of others; while Protestants are believed to be more self-oriented.) The rate busters most often grew up on farms or in small towns, while the conformers came from big cities where they learned loyalty to their peer groups in street gangs. The rate busters were more interested in getting ahead and moving up in the organization than were other workers. Still Dalton's findings do not contradict the Hawthorne ones; most of the workers studied by Dalton, did not break the group norms, and those who did were not integrated members of the work group.

The influence of another non-economic factor on the production rate is best expressed by W. I. Thomas' famous statement: "If men define situations as real, they are real in their consequences." The workers *believed*, on the one hand, that if they worked harder their pay rates would be reduced, and, on the other hand, that if they did not produce a certain amount, they would be unfair to management and might be fired. The conceptions of what management expected implicit in these beliefs influenced the group norm that emerged. But the fact was that management, although it wanted the workers to produce as much as possible, did not have a specific level of production it considered "proper". Thus, although the workers' beliefs had little objective basis, they influenced, if not determined, the level of production in the factory.

3. Often *workers do not act or react as individuals but as members of groups*. Each individual did not feel free to set up for himself a production quota; it was set and enforced by the group. Workers who deviated significantly in either direction from the group norms were penalized by their co-workers. Individual behavior is anchored in the group. A person who will resist pressure to change his behavior as an individual will often change it quite readily if the group of which he is a member changes its behavior. Lewin writes, "As long as group standards are unchanged, the individual will resist changes more strongly the farther he is to depart from group standards. If group standard itself is changed, the resistance which is due to the relation between individual and group standard is eliminated." [4]

The power of the group to produce changes in behavior is analyzed by Lewin in his discussion of experiments on changing eating habits. The experiments were conducted to find out what was the most effective way of getting people to use types of food that they would not ordinarily consider using. Some of the experiments done during World War II attempted to find ways to persuade people to eat kidneys, sweetbreads, and hearts. We will restrict ourselves to an experiment studying how to get mothers to give their children orange juice and codliver oil.[5]

[4] Kurt Lewin, "Group Decision and Social Change," in G. E. Swanson, T. M. Newcomb, and E. L. Hartley (eds.), *Readings in Social Psychology* (New York: Holt, 1952), p. 472.
[5] *Ibid.*, pp. 459–473.

A hospital wanted to convince mothers with newborn children to feed codliver oil and orange juice to their babies immediately following their departure from the hospital. The investigators assigned the mothers one of two types of programs. In the first, a hospital representative talked to each mother singly for about 25 minutes, telling her the virtues of codliver oil and orange juice for her child. In the second program, groups of six mothers discussed with the hospital authority and among themselves the value of the use of these items for their babies. The discussion group also took about 25 minutes.

The results were conclusive. Checking the two samples after two weeks and again after four weeks, the investigators found that the mothers who participated in the discussion group gave their children orange juice and codliver oil much more frequently than the others, although both groups were more inclined to feed their children orange juice than codliver oil. After four weeks, 90 per cent of the mothers who received group instruction were feeding their children codliver oil as compared with about 50 per cent of the mothers who were instructed individually. In the case of orange juice, the comparable figures were 100 per cent and about 58 per cent. Other experiments on changing people's eating habits consistently revealed the same phenomenon: group discussions were much more effective in changing attitudes than other methods, such as two-person discussions or lecture groups.

Management, the Human Relations school concluded, manifestly cannot deal with individual workers as if they were isolated atoms; it must deal with them as members of work groups, subject to the influence of these groups.

4. *The importance of leadership for setting and enforcing group norms and the difference between informal and formal leadership* constitutes another major modification of Scientific Management caused by these studies. Scientific Management tended to assume that the foreman and supervisors would provide the sole leadership of the workers, at least in regard to matters concerning production. In the Bank Wiring Room Study, one of the workers clearly emerged as an informal leader in the group. He was the best liked man in the room and the one who best embodied the norms of his group. More than anyone else his advice was solicited, and to this extent he had the most control over the behavior of his group. He was admired for his ability to "get things done," and he was, to a certain extent, the spokesman of the group to other personnel of the factory. In short, he helped the workers to function as a social group.

In the Bank Wiring Study, the supervisor did not exert a great deal of influence on the work group. In fact, he was under considerable pressure to conform to the norms of the group of which he was supposed to be in charge. Later studies show that a foreman is more likely to be accepted if he exercises what has become known as the Human Relations style of leadership.

One of the earliest and best known studies demonstrating the influence of leadership on a group's behavior is the Lippitt and White study, "Leader-

from human relations to the structuralists

ship and Group Life." [6] This was one of a series of studies begun in the 1930's under the guidance of Kurt Lewin and devised to compare styles of leadership. Three types of leaders were assigned to direct children in arts and crafts work in four different clubs. The first type of leader was *authoritarian*. He was to remain aloof from the group and to use mostly orders in directing the group activities. The *democratic* leader was to offer guiding suggestions, to encourage the children, and to participate in the group. The third type of leader, the *laissez-faire*, supplied knowledge to the group members, but showed little emotional involvement and a minimum of participation in the group activities.

The purpose of the experiment was to observe the general atmosphere of the various groups, to study the effects on the groups and individual members when the leaders were switched, and to find out how the various styles of leadership affected the group activities. The group members were matched for IQ, popularity, energy, etc., and all worked on the same craft project of making masks. Differences among the groups' reactions to various leadership styles were obtained through observations, examination of masks produced, and "experiments," e.g., seeing how the groups reacted when the leader left the room for a specified period.

Great differences were found. The group under democratic leadership manifested warm and friendly relations among the members; members frequently participated in group activities; and, when the leader left the room, the group showed the ability to be independent and to continue working on the project. The democratic group did not produce as much as the authoritarian group, but the quality of their masks was considered higher.

The laissez-faire group did not come off particularly well on either achievement or group satisfaction. Their masks were the poorest; they frequently asked for information from the leader and showed little independence; and their level of group cooperation was low. The investigators found a high level of frustration among group members.

There were two types of reactions on the part of the group to authoritarian leadership. The "aggressive" reaction was rebellious and demanding of the leader's attention. The aggressively reacting children also engaged in scapegoating of other members in the group. The "apathetic" reaction tended to be less critical of the leader. When their group leader was changed to a non-authoritarian one, the "apathetics" were involved in great outbursts of horseplay and emotional release.

Some attempts have been made to apply Lippitt and White's findings to groups in industry to improve the effectiveness of formal leadership (i.e., leadership of those that hold positions in the formal organizational structure, such as foremen). Coch and French showed that democratic-type leadership greatly affects the workers' attitudes toward their jobs.[7] The management of the factory under study had great difficulty in getting the workers to accept technological innovations in the plant. The Harwood Manufac-

---

[6] R. Lippitt and R. K. White, "An Experimental Study of Leadership and Group Life," in Swanson, *et al., Readings in Social Psychology*, pp. 340–355.
[7] L. Coch and J. R. P. French, Jr., "Overcoming Resistance to Change," in Swanson, *et al., Readings in Social Psychology*, pp. 474–490.

37

turing Corporation found that their workers were resisting improvements in the production of pajamas. Coch and French, studying the plant, believed that the resistance might result only in part from the worker's frustration at having to alter established working habits, and that in part it would be accounted for by strong group pressure not to adapt too quickly. The fact that the work groups resisted the change put pressure on each individual member to resist adaptation to the new techniques by keeping production down. To test their hypothesis, Coch and French took a number of workers whose jobs were going to be changed and divided them into three groups, matching the members to assure similarity. The groups were comparable on the basis of prior efficiency, group cohesiveness, and the amount of learning the new job required. The first group was given no orientation to the change other than a short announcement by management that the change would be made. The second group was informed by management of the necessity of the change and of what would be involved, and they were asked to select representatives to help devise the necessary retraining program. The third test group, like the second, was informed of the change and told why it was to occur. But in this case, the whole group participated in helping to design and plan the new jobs as well as the retraining.

The results clearly showed that the two groups that had participated in the orientation, retraining and planning program quickly adjusted to the change while the first group did not. Groups II and III improved their production considerably while in group I production declined. Group III, where there was total participation, did slightly better than group II. Furthermore, while turnover and grievances went up in group I, there was virtually no turnover and no grievances in the other groups.

If these results were not convincing enough, Coch and French did a follow-up study with group I. Several months later the members of group I were compelled to change their jobs again, but this time they participated in a program similar to that of group III in the previous experiment. They showed the same successful adaptation to the change that group III had demonstrated, by increasing their production and group satisfaction. This result denies the possibility that their previous maladjustment had been due to personality factors among the members of the group.

5. Following these experiments, and the writings of Mayo and Lewin, the Human Relations approach came to emphasize the importance of *communication between the ranks*, of explaining to the lower participants the reasons why a particular course of action is taken; the importance of *participation in decision-making* in which lower ranks share in the decisions made by higher ranks, in particular in matters that affect them directly; and the virtues of *democratic leadership* which not only is highly communicative and encourages participation but also is just, non-arbitrary and concerned with the problems of workers, not just those of work.

There are few social science studies and insights that have received more attention or were more widely reported in popular literature and in the trade manuals than these experiments and the conclusions Human Relations drew from them. Many thousands of executives and lower ranking supervisors have participated in Human Relations workshops or have taken

from human relations to the structuralists

some type of instruction in which these materials were expounded. Although there have unquestionably been many factors other than the Human Relations school which have influenced the character of American management, and although no one has documented just how influential the Human Relations educational efforts have been, American management—and to some degree management in other industrial societies—clearly has changed its thoughts and habits under the influence of this approach.[8] The Human Relations approach is still widely accepted in managerial circles.

Conclusion

Scientific Management and Human Relations were in many ways diametrically opposed. The factors one school saw as critical and crucial, the other hardly considered, and the variables one viewed as central, the other largely ignored. The two schools however had one element in common: neither saw any basic contradiction or insoluble dilemma in the relationship between the organization's quest for rationality and the human search for happiness. Scientific Management assumed that the most efficient organization would also be the most satisfying one, since it would maximize both productivity and the workers' pay. Since the worker was viewed as an economic man seeking to maximize his income, and since it was assumed that he was satisfied with his share of the corporate income, the implicit belief was maintained that what is best for the organization is best for the workers and *vice versa*. In this sense, Scientific Management is the organization's counterpart of the perfect competition theory of the economic market which assumes that perfect competition (the rational state) maximizes both the welfare of the economy and of the various participating units.

The Human Relations approach assumed that the most satisfying organization would be the most efficient. It suggested that the workers would not be happy in the cold, formal, "rational" organization that satisfied only their economic needs. The Human Relations school did not believe that management would be able to establish an organization that would keep the workers satisfied by simply allocating labor and authority in the most efficient way as determined by the intrinsic nature of the task. But, like Scientific Management, it did not view the problem of worker satisfaction and productivity as inherently unsolvable. True, management had to be enlightened and certain steps had to be taken, such as encouraging the development of social groups on-the-job and providing them with democratic, participating, and communicative leadership; but once the real nature of the workers' needs and their informal group life and organizations are understood, nothing prevents management from making the organizational life a happy one.

Moreover, the Human Relations school taught that it is necessary to relate work and the organizational structure to the social needs of the employees, for in this way, by making the employee happy, the organization would obtain their full cooperation and effort and thus increase its efficiency.

[8] Reinhard Bendix, *Work and Authority in Industry* (New York: Wiley, 1956), pp. 319ff.

from human relations to the structuralists

Thus the way to make the organization fully rational was to increase by deliberate efforts the happiness of the workers. There are many almost lyric pages in Human Relations writing which depict the worker as anxious not to miss a day at the factory or to come too late lest he miss spending some time with his friends, and even as anxious not to disappoint his foreman who is like a warm and understanding father to him. The work team itself is often referred to as a family. The Human Relations approach maintained that "employees should have a feeling that the company's 'goal is worth their effort; they should feel themselves part of the company and take pride in their contribution to its goal. This means that the company's objectives must be such as to inspire confidence in the intentions of management and belief that each will get rewards and satisfactions by working for these objectives." [9]

In short, the Human Relations school pointed to a perfect balance between the organization's goals and the workers' needs. The two views were only different in substance of the balance they depicted: whereas Scientific Management saw the balance as natural if restraints were removed, Human Relations believed the ideal state had to be deliberately constructed. Implicit in many Human Relations writings is the suggestion that the task of the social scientist is to show management how to engage in the art of social engineering to the benefit of all concerned. It remained, therefore, for the Structuralists to point out that alienation and conflict are both inevitable and occasionally desirable, and to emphasize that social science is not a vehicle to serve the needs of either worker or organization. It is no more concerned to improve the organization of management than it is to improve organization of the employees.

Two key related concepts that have emerged from the Scientific Management and Human Relations schools have remained central to organizational studies no matter how they have been guided—by one of the organizational traditions or by none. These are the concepts of formal and informal organization. The former derives from the set of factors considered crucial by Scientific Management, and the latter from those stressed by Human Relations. *Formal organization* generally refers to the organizational pattern designed by management: the blueprint of division of labor and power of control, the rules and regulations about wages, fines, quality control, etc. *Informal organization* refers either to the social relations that develop among the staff or workers above and beyond the formal one determined by the organization (e.g., they not only work as a team on the same machine but are also friends), or to the actual organizational relations as they evolved as a consequence of the interaction between the organizational design and the pressures of the interpersonal relations among the participants (e.g., formally no worker should leave the plant before five o'clock but it is informally accepted that on Fridays it is "all right" for the secretaries to leave at 4:45 since all the other office employees do). A discussion of formal organization brings to mind questions of relations between organizational divisions or ranks; informal organization suggests peer groups and their members, and relations between leaders and followers in those groups. It was left

[9] Burleigh B. Gardner, *Human Relations in Industry* (Chicago: Irwin, 1945), p. 283.

40

largely to the Structuralist school to raise systematically the question of the relationship between formal and informal organizations.

The Structuralist Critique

Having many sources but only one adversary, the Structuralist approach is a synthesis of the Classical (or formal) school and the Human Relations (or informal) one, drawing also on the work of Max Weber, and, to a degree, that of Karl Marx. But its major dialogue has been with the Human Relations approach. Its foundations are best understood through examination of the criticism it raised against this school. It is in exploring the "harmony" view of the Human Relations writers that the Structuralist writers first recognize fully the organizational dilemma: the inevitable strains—which can be reduced but not eliminated—between organizational needs and personal needs; between rationality and non-rationality; between discipline and autonomy; between formal and informal relations; between management and workers, or, more generically, between ranks and divisions. Whereas Human Relations concentrated on industrial and business organizations, the Structuralists studied in addition hospitals and prisons, churches and armies, social-work agencies and schools, enlarging the scope of organizational analysis to match that of the existing organizational types. In this section we examine the growth of the Structuralist approach as a response to Human Relations in which some of the major tenets of the latter were absorbed into the more encompassing frame of reference of the former. The following chapter deals with the greatest Structuralist writer; and the rest of the volume is largely written in terms of the synthesis this approach provided.

The Organizational System

The Structuralists suggested that the Human Relations approach did not provide a full view of the organization and that its partial view favors management and misleads the workers.[10] The Structuralist sees the organization as a large, complex social unit in which many social groups interact. While these groups share some interests (e.g., in the economic viability of the corporation) they have other, incompatible interests (e.g., in how the gross profits of the organization are to be distributed). They share some values, especially national ones, whose influence becomes evident in periods of international crisis, but they disagree on many others, as for example their evaluations of the place of labor in the society. The various groups might cooperate in some spheres and compete in others, but they hardly are or can become one big happy family as Human Relations writers often imply.

Two groups within the organization whose interests frequently come into conflict are management and the workers. This is largely because management's effort to get him to work is basically alienating to the worker.

---

[10] Reinhard Bendix and Lloyd H. Fisher, "The Perspectives of Elton Mayo," Amitai Etzioni (ed.), *Complex Organizations: A Sociological Reader* (New York: Holt, Rinehart and Winston, 1961) pp. 113–126.

There are many ways to make labor more pleasant, but none to make it satisfying in any absolute sense. The Structuralists accepted this viewpoint and, following the analyses of Marx and Weber, they sought in the contrast between the medieval artisan or farmer and the modern worker some clues to the source of the latter's dissatisfaction.

According to Marx, the modern factory hand is alienated from his work since he owns neither the means of production nor the product of his labor. Specialization has fragmented production so that each worker's labor has become repetitious, monotonous, and lacks opportunity for creativity and self-expression. The worker has little conception of the whole work process or of his contribution to it; his work is meaningless. He has little control over the time at which his work starts and stops or over the pace at which it is carried out. To this Marxian analysis, Weber added that this basic estrangement exists not only between the worker and the means of production, but also between the soldier and the means of warfare, the scientist and the means of inquiry, etc. This is not just a legal question of ownership (e.g., that the gun belongs to the army and not to the soldier), but rather that with ownership goes the right to control, and that those that provide the means also define their use; thus the worker, soldier, and researcher—and by implication all employees of all organizations—are frustrated, unhappy since they cannot determine what use their efforts will be put to since they do not own the instrument necessary to carry out independently the work that needs to be done. When asked, "all said and done, how satisfied are you with your work?" about 80 per cent of American blue-collar workers answer "not satisfied." [11] Alienation is a concept that stands for this sentiment and the analysis of its source in the Marxian-Weberian terms.

To be sure, the Human Relations approach has indicated some ways in which the resulting frustrations might be reduced, but, the Structuralists insist, there are sharp limits on the degree to which this can be achieved. The development of social groups on the job might make the worker's day more pleasant, but it does not make his task any the less repetitious or uncreative. Similarly, rotation eases the problem of monotony but does not change its basic nature since rotation is limited by the scope of the alternative jobs available, all similar in their dull, routine and meaningless nature. Workers, it is suggested, spend much of their working day in a semi-conscious delirium, dreaming about their major source of satisfaction, the post-work day.[12]

By providing an unrealistic "happy" picture, by viewing the factory as a family rather than as a power struggle among groups with some conflicting values and interests as well as some shared ones, and by seeing it as a major source of human satisfaction rather than alienation, Human Relations comes to gloss over the realities of work life. Worker dissatisfaction is viewed as indicative of lack of understanding of the situation rather than as symptomatic of any underlying real conflict of interests. Although Warner and Low, in their study of a strike in a shoe factory were not unaware of the

[11] See various studies cited in F. Herzberg, *et al.*, *Job Attitudes* (Pittsburgh: Psychological Service, 1957).

[12] Eli Chinoy, *Automobile Workers and the American Dream* (New York: Doubleday, 1955).

from human relations to the structuralists

workers' desire for higher wages in a situation where wages had been severely reduced, they saw as the underlying factors in the conflict the workers' loss of a sense of community, decline in primary relations, and communication blocks between management and workers.[13] "In the early days of the shoe industry, the owners and managerial staffs of the factories, as well as the operatives, were residents of Yankee City; there was no extension of the factory social structures outside the local community. The factories were then entirely under the control of the community: not only the formal control of city ordinances and laws, but also the more pervasive informal controls of community traditions and attitudes. There were feelings of neighborliness and friendship between manager and worker and of mutual responsibilities to each other and to the community that went beyond the formal employer-employee agreement."[14] As the vertical hierarchy of the factory system extended to executive offices in New York, even the local factory managers came to be, for the most part, "outsiders." The workers knew or felt that the forces that controlled local men would not control these outsiders. The vast network of relations and memberships that made the former owners local leaders, as well as local manufacturers, had been reduced to a purely economic one of employer and employee."[15]

It is to this partial approach with its underplaying of the importance of material rewards that the Structuralists objected. The Structuralists accepted, however, although with some lessening of emphasis, the Human Relations insights into the significance of social rewards in industry, but they criticized the use to which these insights were put in those instances in which management sought to placate the workers by granting them inexpensive symbols of prestige and affection instead of an increase in wages.

The differences in approach may be highlighted in the following case. In a typical Human Relations training movie we see a happy factory in which the wheels hum steadily and the workers rhythmically serve the machines with smiles on their faces. A truck arrives and unloads large crates containing new machines. A dark type with long sideburns who sweeps the floors in the factory spreads a rumor that mass firing is imminent since the new machines will take over the work of many of the workers. The wheels turn slower, the workers are sad. In the evening they carry their gloom to their suburban homes. The next morning, the reassuring voice of their boss comes over the inter-com. He tells them that the rumor is absolutely false; the machines are to be set up in a new wing and more workers will be hired since the factory is expanding its production. Everybody sighs in relief, smiles return, the machines hum speedily and steadily again. Only the dark floor sweeper is sad. Nobody will listen to his rumors anymore. The moral is clear: had management been careful to communicate its development plans to its workers, the crisis would have been averted. Once it occurred, increase in communication eliminated it like magic.

The Structuralist would not question the validity of this training movie.

[13] W. Lloyd Warner and J. O. Low, *The Social System of the Modern Factory* (New Haven: Yale University Press, 1947).
[14] *Ibid.*, p. 108.
[15] W. Lloyd Warner and J. O. Low, "The Factory in the Community," in William F. Whyte (ed.), *Industry and Society* (New York: McGraw-Hill, 1946), p. 40.

Problems initially created by false communication (the floor sweeper rumor) and by lack of authentic communication can be eliminated or at least largely reduced through increase in authentic communication. The question the Structuralist is compelled to raise is what would management have done if the rumor were correct, if it was forced to reduce its labor force, let us say, because of automation? Even here communication might have somewhat eased the situation by clarifying the extent of the expected firings and the procedure to be followed, but surely it could not have eliminated or even significantly reduced the alienation of those to be fired, and of many of their friends whose turn might come next. Differences in economic interests and power positions cannot be communicated away.

Industrial conflict is viewed by many social scientists of the older generation and by most Human Relations writers as basically undesirable. The Human Relations experts seek to promote industrial harmony. The Structuralists, however, point to the many important social functions of conflict, including its positive contributions for the organizational system itself,[16] and object to any artificial smothering of conflict. The expression of conflict allows genuine differences of interests and beliefs to emerge, whose confrontation may lead to a test of power and adjustment of the organizational system to the real situation, and ultimately to organizational peace. If glossed over, conflict and its concomitant latent alienation will seek other outlets such as withdrawal or increase in accidents which in the end are disadvantageous to both worker and organization.

The Manipulative Charge

An anthropologist recorded the following conversation in a mental hospital. It involved the medical director, the administrative director, and a nurse, and it concerned sessions in which patients were encouraged to express their dissatisfactions with hospital routines.

> MISS NUGENT *nurse:* Are you going to have a gripe session?
>
> DR. SCOTT: I'm personally against these gripe sessions.
>
> DR. SHAW: So am I, particularly if the patients feel that they are legislating at these sessions, and find out later that they are not.
>
> DR. SCOTT: The only good that these gripe sessions do is that if you can get the patients as a group to scrutinize what is going on in their behavior. . . .[17]

Here, conferences (gripe sessions) which patients were led to believe were being held to provide an opportunity for upward communication were actually used for purposes of downward communication and direction. Such "manipulation" is objectionable to many Structuralists, although here their opposition might be somewhat less intense since these manipulations had therapeutic intent, and this was after all a hospital. But in most other organizations, and especially in industrial organizations, such manipulation, it

16 Lewis Coser, *The Social Functions of Conflict* (Glencoe, Illinois: The Free Press, 1956).

17 William Caudill, *The Psychiatric Hospital as a Small Society* (Cambridge: Harvard University Press, 1958), p. 78.

from human relations to the structuralists

has been asserted, is unethical; here Human Relations techniques are utilized to help those higher in rank manipulate the lower in rank.

Two Human Relations consultants, under the title "Group Participation," make the following point:

> Managements look with skepticism on group methods which integrate conflict and utilize maximum participation, because they are a departure from custom. The president of an organization said, "Do you mean to tell me a stock boy can help me manage my business?" It is certainly not impossible that the stock boy could give the president some ideas, but the president is thinking of the stock boy sitting on the board of directors. This is not intended, and anyway the stock boy would be extremely uncomfortable. But a visit with the stock boy and some of his fellow workers for an exchange of opinions and experience would give the president some idea of *how to manage* the stock boys.[18] (Italics added.)

Those lower in rank might be invited to participate in "democratic" discussions leading to joint decision-making, when in fact the decisions have already been made and the real purpose of the conference is to get the lower in rank to accept them. Or the lower in rank are allowed to decide on relatively unimportant matters whose outcome is of indifference to top management. What is created here is a false sense of participation and autonomy which has been deliberately induced in order to elicit the workers' cooperation in and commitment to organizational enterprise. Thus it has been charged that providing workers with "gripe sessions" and suggestion boxes, with social workers and psychiatric interviews, as is done in some Human Relations programs, may reduce their alienation without improving their lot. The Human Relations proponents counter that they do not favor one group over another; that their findings are public and hence anyone—including both workers and management—may have access to them (indeed some union leaders have taken courses in order to improve their control of their membership). The Human Relations writers point out that workers and management try to manipulate each other anyhow, and that the study of manipulation did not create it. Moreover, most social-science studies are open to use by "manipulators" since they provide readers with insights into the structure and dynamics of social processes which might be used to the disadvantage (or advantage) of others. Furthermore, only the most biased observer would deny that increased communication and participation and the granting of social rewards—even without wage increases—have improved the workers' life and job. Finally, one must recognize that many plants which have Human Relations· programs are among those in which pay is highest, working conditions best, and unions most accepted. The use of the Human Relations approach may improve the worker's social situation without sacrificing his economic interests.

Multifactor Approach

1. *Formal and informal.* The major analytical rather than ideological criticism of the Human Relations approach is that it tends

---

[18] Elizabeth and Francis Jennings, "Making Human Relations Work," in Edward C. Bursk (ed.), *Human Relations for Management* (New York: Harper, 1956), p. 81.

to focus on a narrow range of variables and to study them without taking others into account. It often fails to relate the findings on the variables studied in a particular study to those examined elsewhere. Thus the Human Relations people tend to devote much attention to informal relations among workers and between workers and supervisors, but little to the formal ones or to the articulation of formal relationships with informal ones. It is true that workers form informal groups, but how do these relate to the formal organization? Are all or most or only few of the workers in any one work unit also members of one informal group? Do informal groups cut across formal divisions or do they tend to parallel them? Are informal groups equally likely to evolve in all organizational ranks and divisions, or are they more likely in some than in others? It is true that informal groups respond to leadership, but under what conditions is this leadership provided by formal leaders who have organizational (i.e., informal leaders) positions? Are there cases where leadership is divided between formal and informal leaders? If so, how does such division affect organizational rationality and the workers' commitment or alienation? A careful reading of various Human Relations descriptive accounts of work relations does provide considerable material on the relationships between the informal factors which the Human Relations experts focus on and the formal factors which they tend to underplay. Most of all, there is little systematic effort to relate the two sets of factors. This has been mainly a contribution of the Structuralist school.

2. *The scope of informal groups.* Many Human Relations studies have pointed to the existence of informal groups in industry and to their psychological and sociological significance especially in view of the disintegration of social life outside the factory under the impact of industrialization. But there are very few Human Relations studies which ask how common such informal work groups are, how rare off-the-job groups are, and what their relative importance actually is. The Structuralists in their organizational researches found that informal work groups are not so common and the majority of workers do not belong to any. Dubin, in his survey of the "central life interests" of 1,200 industrial workers, found that "only 9 per cent of the industrial workers in the sample preferred the informal group life that is centered in the job." [19] He added that "In particular, work is not a central life interest for industrial workers when we studied the informal group experiences and the general social experiences that have some affective value for them . . . ." [20] A study by Walker and Guest of 179 assembly line workers showed that there were virtually no social groups on the job.[21] Vollmer reported that 53 per cent of male skilled workers had "no co-workers as close friends outside work." [22]

Mayo and many of his associates expected the atomization of society

[19] Robert Dubin, "Industrial Workers' Worlds: A Study of the 'Central Life Interests' of Industrial Workers," *Social Problems* (1956), 4:136.

[20] *Ibid.*, p. 140.

[21] C. R. Walker and R. H. Guest, *The Man on the Assembly Line* (Cambridge: Harvard University Press, 1952).

[22] H. M. Vollmer, *Employer Rights and the Employment Relationship* (Berkeley and Los Angeles: University of California Press, 1960), p. 75.

from human relations to the structuralists

as a result of industrialization. Industrialization, they thought, would lead to disintegration of traditional social groups such as the family, village community and religious groups. They predicted the disappearance of the intermediary bodies between the state and the individual as mass society evolved. Hence they saw the mission of the new social unit, the factory, as providing a new home, a place of emotional security for the atomized individual. Management was expected to provide the needed social and emotional shelters, and in return it would be rewarded with a devoted, hardworking and satisfied labor force. In fact, the traditional social groups did decline in importance, scope, and degree of integration. The typical modern family is smaller in size, less stable, and socially less prominent than the traditional one. Many rural communities and religious groups have similarly declined. But most of these groups have not disappeared. After a long period of descent their decline has stopped and has been partially reversed. Over the last two decades the family has experienced a resurgence in social evaluation if not in stability. The same holds for religion and the religious groups. Moreover, new bases of social relations have developed, especially in urban and even more in suburban ecological units. Labor unions provide some social life outside the factory. Thus, by and large, the modern worker does not come to the factory starved for affection and affiliation. Some old and some new social units provide for most, if not all, of his gregarious needs. It is therefore not surprising to find that informal groups are not common among workers. They are somewhat more common among higher organizational ranks (rarely studied by the Human Relations school) where both social and geographical mobility reduce the social ties of a person to his parental family, initial residential community, and friends; hence he tends to rely more heavily on social ties found at work.[23] It is at this level that Mayo's insight can be most fruitfully applied.

3. *The organization and its environment.* The typical Human Relations study approaches the informal work group in the factory, and sometimes the factory as a whole, as an island to be studied the way anthropologists study a self-contained tribe. Not all Structuralists refrained from this limitation of perspective; more recently, however, increasing attention has been paid to processes in the environment that affect the organization most intimately, and to processes within the organization that affect its relations with the environment, such as contacts with clients, interaction among organizations, and between organizations and higher power structures such as the government. Particularly important are the effects of multi-group membership of workers and other participants, both within and without the organization. We will return to this subject below in our discussion of the organization and its environment (see Chapter 10).

4. *Material and social reward.* The Structuralists view the Scientific Management and Human Relations approaches to rewards as segmental; in the Structuralist tradition, the study of both is combined. The significance of social rewards, of affection and esteem, has been demonstrated beyond doubt. Lawyers are known to have given up 6-digit incomes to become

[23] William H. Whyte, Jr., *The Organization Man* (Garden City, New York: Doubleday, 1957).

from human relations to the structuralists

judges at 5-digit salaries, "compensated" by the higher prestige of the bench. Vice-presidents, miserable at being passed over when a new president was appointed, have become far less miserable when they also were "promoted" by having their title changed to that of executive-vice-president. Everything that is included under status symbols—office size, assigned places in the company's parking lot, and so on—is important in the life of any organization. But one must realize that for symbolic rewards to be effective, the recipient must first identify with the granting organization and, even more important, the symbols must be appreciated by the recipient's "significant others" [24]—by his wife, his friends, his neighbors. For these reasons, social rewards are less effective in controlling blue-collar than white-collar workers, and low-ranking than high-ranking employees. For a blue-collar worker, official recognition by management might well be a source of deprivation, because co-workers may ridicule or ostracize him. The same holds for the "teacher's pet" in schools, for "favored" inmates in prisons, or for "soldier of the month" in the army.

Although social rewards have been proven important in organizations, this does not reduce the importance of material rewards. A survey conducted by the federal government of 514 plants where wage incentive plans were introduced showed that, on the average, production increased 38.99 per cent and labor costs decreased 11.58 per cent.[25] In another case, an hourly wage differential of about 30 per cent led many steel workers to exchange their comparatively non-repetitive, skilled, autonomous jobs for assembly-line jobs which lacked these qualities but paid more.[26]

5. *Factories, churches, prisons and schools.* While Human Relations and Scientific Management focused almost exclusively on organizations such as factories, banks, and insurance companies, the Structuralist approach broadened the scope of organizational analysis to include a large variety of organizations from the Communist party to the Catholic Church, and from a maximum-security prison to a small residential college. Thus, not only have the contributions of the two earlier approaches been incorporated in the Structuralist approach, but additional factors not previously studied are considered and the full range of organizations is covered.

The great synthesis is far from universal: There are still Human Relations training manuals whose authors have learned little and forgotten little since Mayo wrote his first books; and though fewer in number, there are still some "pure" studies of administration in the old formalistic sense. Generally, however, those who still identify themselves with one or the other of these earlier schools have come to broaden their theoretical approach, and are moving in the general direction of the synthesis suggested in the preceding pages.[27]

[24] On this concept see G. H. Mead, *Mind, Self and Society* (Chicago: University of Chicago Press, 1934).

[25] M. S. Viteles, *Motivation and Morale to Industry* (New York: Norton, 1953), p. 27.

[26] Walker and Guest, *The Man on the Assembly Line*, p. 91.

[27] For two fine reviews of such development in the Human Relations tradition, see William F. Whyte, "Human Relations Theory: A Progress Report," *Harvard Business Review*, 24 (1956), 34:125–132; and Rensis Likert, *New Patterns of Management* (New York: McGraw-Hill, 1962).

from human relations to the structuralists

In general, organizational analysis has broadened its concerns to include:

1. both formal and informal elements of the organization and their articulation;
2. the scope of informal groups and the relations between such groups inside and outside the organization;
3. both lower and higher ranks;
4. both social and material rewards and their effects on each other;
5. the interaction between the organization and its environment;
6. both work and non-work organizations.

This more encompassing and balanced perspective not only encourages the growth of a value-free, neither pro-management nor pro-worker, approach to organizational analysis and the expansion of its scope to include all types of organizations and all the elements of organization, but it enriches the study of any single element by providing a context within which to place it, and points of reference for judging its importance to the organization.

bureaucracies:
structure
and legitimation
five

Max Weber, most influential of the Structuralist founders, was very concerned with the distribution of power among the organizational positions in the bureaucratic structure, and this represents the "formal" element of his work. At the same time, in his exploration of legitimation, he opened up a whole new perspective on the study of satisfaction derived from participation in the organization. His insights on the interplay between the power to control and the ability to justify ("legitimize") its use set the context for a great deal of the following work on the central organizational question: how to control the participants so as to maximize effectiveness and efficiency and minimize the unhappiness this very need to control produces.

To what extent can the organization expect its participants to accept its rulings because "they always were so," to what extent because the rulings agree with a law the participants acknowledge, and to what degree must the person who issues an order be highly persuasive? What characterizes the more rational power structures? What service do non-rational elements perform for the rational ones? And what effects does the departure of the "charismatic leader," the focus of the non-rational commitments and the ultimate source of legitimation, have on the participants, and hence on the organization's ability to control them? This chapter discusses Weber's contribution to these subjects; the following chapters review studies of organizational control that have largely been constructed on the foundations he laid.

50

Legitimation and Authority

Organizations, which Weber referred to as bureaucracies, set norms and need to enforce them; they have rules and regulations and issue orders, which must be obeyed if the organization is to function effectively. To a degree, an organization can rely on its power to make the participant obey. That is, it can use some of its resources to reward those who follow its rulings and to penalize those who do not. Such discipline does not require that the recipient of the order agree with it, and certainly not that he accept it as morally justified. He may follow an order to avoid loss of money or prestige and to increase his income or status. To some extent, the organization can maintain discipline by manipulating various rewards and sanctions in order to ensure maximum contentment and minimize disappointment.

The exercise of power, however, has a major limitation: It keeps the subject, as he conforms, alienated. He conforms because of ulterior motives. His conformity is likely to be limited to the matters explicitly backed by power. He will be unlikely to volunteer information, show initiative, or cooperate, except when he is explicitly forced to. Moreover, in moments of crisis, when the power structure of the organization is weakened, he will tend to prefer whatever other norms he subscribes to rather than the organization's.

On the other hand, when the exercise of power is seen as legitimate by those subject to it—that is, when the orders issued or rules set conform to the values to which the subjects are committed—compliance will be much deeper and more effective. The subject will "internalize" the rules. He will find the discipline less alienating, and he will continue to follow rules and orders when the organization's power is weakened or even absent.

It is crucial to realize the nature of the power increment which legitimation bestows. It does not increase the material interest of the subordinate in compliance; it does not make the order or rule necessarily pleasant —i.e., gratifying to the subject. But it fulfills a third kind of need, the need to follow norms which match rather than conflict with one's values. In order to emphasize the difference between normative satisfaction of the need for justice (or legitimacy) and the need to find opportunities to gratify other needs, which are often confused, it is important to realize that whereas some legitimate orders are gratifying, many other orders may be legitimate and not gratifying, or still others may be illegitimate yet gratifying. Thus Weber's study of legitimation introduces a whole new dimension to the study of organizational discipline. He used *power* to refer to the ability to induce acceptance of orders; *legitimation* to refer to the acceptance of the exercise of power because it is in line with values held by the subjects; and *authority* to refer to the combination of the two—i.e., to power that is viewed as legitimate.

Weber's Typology of Authority

Weber's typology of authority is based on the sources and kinds of legitimation employed rather than on the types of power applied. He referred to authority as *traditional* when the subjects accept the

bureaucracies: structure and legitimation

orders of superiors as justified on the grounds that this is the way things are always done; and as rational-legal, or *bureaucratic*, when the subjects accept a ruling as justified because it agrees with a set of more abstract rules which they consider legitimate, and from which the ruling is "derived" (and, in this sense, is rational). (The work of the Roman courts is a fine example.) Finally, Weber pointed to charismatic authority in which the subjects accept a superior's orders as justified because of the influence of his personality, with which they identify.

Weber's classification of authority may be applied on at least three levels. One might apply it on the societal level, comparing traditional, bureaucratic, and charismatic societies. The medieval society is often viewed as traditional, the modern democratic as bureaucratic, and societies in revolutionary periods—such as Russia after 1917 and Nazi Germany in the years following 1933—as charismatic. One might compare different kinds of social units according to type of authority base. Here the family is seen as traditional (even in a bureaucratic society), complex organizations as bureaucratic (even in a charismatic period), and revolutionary political parties as charismatic (even in a traditional society). Finally, one might use the breakdown to characterize relations between individual subjects and their superiors within a given organization.

Moreover, different authority relations tend to arise in different social structures. Traditional authority relations are typically found in a diffuse status structure where a superior in one realm is a superior in others, as for example in an aristocracy. Authority relations in bureaucratic structures are limited in scope; superiority is not transferred from one social realm to another. In the case of pure charismatic relations, not only is there no differentiation between the organizational and other social units, but there is little internal differentiation between the leader and the followers.

Weber suggested that to be effective and efficient as an organizational instrument, a modern organizational structure requires bureaucratic authority. Charismatic relations lack any systematic division of labor, specialization, or stability. Organizational activities in traditional social units are not sufficiently immune from nonrelevant political, stratification, and kinship considerations, and hence do not allow the rationality of the productive or administrative process to exert itself. Only where the scope of the organization is low (see below, Chapter 7) does immunity from irrelevant factors, freedom to structure relations according to the requirements of a task, and acceptance of the rules on permanent grounds, all essential to modern organization, emerge. Hence, bureaucracies are the social units most suited for rational, modern organization.

Yet Weber was aware of the fragility of the rational structure. Not only are there constant pressures from outside forces to encourage the bureaucrat to follow norms other than those of the organization, but the subject's commitment to the bureaucratic rules tends itself to decline. Here is a typical organizational dilemma. For the organization to be effective, it requires a special kind of legitimation, rationality, and narrowness of scope. But the ability to accept orders and rules as legitimate, particularly when they are repugnant to one's desires—frequently the case in bureaucracies—requires a level of self-denial that is difficult to maintain. Hence bureau-

bureaucracies: structure and legitimation

cratic organizations tend to break either in the charismatic or the traditional direction where discipline relations are less separated from other, more "natural", "warmer" ones. Moreover, the capacity for self-denial which the rational organization requires cannot be developed within it; it depends upon the more encompassing social relationships that exist in the traditional family or charismatic movement. Weber traced the origin of bureaucracies in earlier social units of these types, a point to which we will return once the nature of the bureaucratic structure is spelled out.

The Bureaucratic Structure

Weber spelled out in considerable detail the features of the bureaucratic structure. They all specify what makes a highly rational structure.[1]

1. "A continuous organization of official functions bound by *rules*." Rational organization is the antithesis of ad hoc, temporary, unstable relations; hence the stress on continuity. Rules save effort by obviating the need for deriving a new solution for every problem and case; they facilitate standardization and equality in the treatment of many cases. These advantages are impossible if each client is treated as a unique case, as an individual.

2. "A specific sphere of competence. This involves (a) a sphere of obligations to perform functions which have been marked off as part of a systematic division of labor; (b) the provision of the incumbent with the necessary authority to carry out these functions; and (c) that the necessary means of compulsion are clearly defined and their use is subject to definite conditions." Thus a systematic division of labor, rights, and power is essential for rational organization. Not only must each participant know his job and have the means to carry it out, which includes first of all the ability to command others, but he also must know the limits of his job, rights, and power so as not to overstep the boundaries between his role and those of others and thus undermine the whole structure.

3. "The organization of offices follows the principle of hierarchy; that is, each lower office is under the control and supervision of a higher one." In this way no office is left uncontrolled. Compliance cannot be left to chance; it has to be systematically checked and reinforced.

4. "The rules which regulate the conduct of an office may be *technical* rules or norms. In both cases, if their application is to be fully rational, specialized training is necessary. It is thus normally true that only a person who has demonstrated an adequate technical training is qualified to be a member of the administrative staff . . . ." We examine below (in Chapter 9) the full import of this statement by Weber. It suffices to say here that he thought that the root of the authority of the bureaucrat is his knowledge and his training. Not that these replace legitimation, but his command of

<hr>

[1] Max Weber (Talcott Parsons, ed.; A. M. Henderson and Talcott Parsons, trans.), *The Theory of Social and Economic Organization* (New York: Oxford University Press, 1947), pp. 329–330. Reprinted in Robert K. Merton, Ailsa P. Gray, Barbara Hockey, and Hanan C. Selvin (eds.), *Reader in Bureaucracy* (Glencoe, Ill.: The Free Press, 1952), pp. 18–20.

technical skill and knowledge is the basis on which legitimation is granted to him.

5. "It is a matter of principle that the members of the administrative staff should be completely separated from ownership of the means of production or administration. . . . There exists, furthermore, in principle, complete separation of the property belonging to the organization, which is controlled within the spheres of the office, and the personal property of the official . . . ." This segregation, which Weber applied to other elements of the status, such as the segregation of the bureaucrat's personal residence from the organization, keeps the official's bureaucratic status from being infringed by the demands of his non-organizational statuses.

6. In order to enhance this organizational freedom, the resources of the organization have to be free of any outside control and the positions cannot be monopolized by any incumbent. They have to be free to be allocated and re-allocated according to the needs of the organization. "A complete *absence* of appropriation of his official positions by the incumbent" is required.

7. "Administrative acts, decisions, and rules are formulated and recorded in writing . . . ." Most observers might view this requirement as less essential or basic to rational organization than the preceding ones, and many will point to the irrationality of keeping excessive records, files, and the like, often referred to as "red tape." Weber, however, stressed the need to maintain a systematic interpretation of norms and enforcement of rules, which cannot be maintained through oral communication.

Weber pointed out that officials should be compensated by salaries and not receive payments from clients to ensure that their primary orientation be to the organization, to its norms and representatives. Moreover, by promoting officials systematically, thus channeling their ambitions by providing them with careers, and by rewarding those loyal to it, the corporation would reinforce this commitment.

Underlying the whole analysis is a set of principles that follows from the central organizational problem as Weber saw it: The high rationality of the bureaucratic structure is fragile; it needs to be constantly protected against external pressures to safeguard the autonomy required if it is to be kept closely geared to its goals and not others.

The Non-bureaucratic Head

The rules Weber specified are concerned with relationships between bureaucrats—i.e., those who make up the administrative body of the organizational hierarchy and structure. But, Weber indicated, organizations have non-bureaucratic heads. Although the bureaucrats follow the rules, the head sets them; although the administrative body serves the organization's goals, the head decides which goals are to be served; although the bureaucrats are appointed, the head is often elected or inherits his position. Presidents, cabinets, boards of trustees, and kings are typical non-bureaucratic heads of bureaucratic organizations.

These organizational heads fulfill an important function in helping to maintain the emotional (and in this sense, non-rational) commitment to

bureaucracies: structure and legitimation

rationality. Most mortals find it difficult to maintain a commitment to an abstract set of norms and rules, especially as these run counter to the extra-organizational relations which pressure the bureaucrat to make irrelevant (to the organization) preferences, such as acting on kinship, local, political, racial, religious, or ethnic considerations rather than on the criteria set by the organization. Identification with a person, a leader, or with the head of the organization provides the psychological leverage that reinforces abstract commitment to the rules of the organizations, by providing a more concrete and "warm" image with whom it is easier to identify.

Weber viewed some bureaucracies as emerging historically from charismatic movements—e.g., the Church from the early Christian communities, and the Soviet state from the Communist movement. The founder of the movement, the great charismatic, is also the spiritual father of the new structure. He bestows his light on it and, by blessing the new structure, transfers to it some of the commitment of his followers. The successors to the charismatic head, as Weber saw them, are like the moon which reflects the light of the sun. They have little or no charisma of their own, but maintain the commitment of the lower ranks by acquiring charisma from the office they occupy. Thus the popes are viewed as representing Jesus, and are endowed with some of his charismatic power.

These secondary leaders, according to Weber, never match the founder in charisma; on the contrary, they gradually use up the stock of charisma which the top office has acquired from the founder until the stock of charisma is exhausted and the structure loses its legitimacy. Then, according to Weber's theory of history, the unit—whether the society or a bureaucracy—disintegrates, the final blow being dealt by a new charismatic leader who emerges from the old structure and topples it by means of a revolutionary movement from which a new structure develops, built on the ruins of the old one.

The Succession Crisis

According to Weber's model, the rational commitment of the lower in rank to those higher in rank, and to the organization in general, makes most higher-ranking individual participants "dispensable." As long as the individual who leaves or dies is replaced by one with similar technical qualifications, the organization's effectiveness should not be impaired. Commitments are to the position, not to the incumbent, and should hence be easy to transfer. Only the departure or death of the non-bureaucratic head of an organization, the one person to whom commitments are personal rather than bureaucratic, involves a major organizational crisis. The succession crisis is particularly evident in totalitarian states, and there almost invariably leads to a period of instability. But corporations, churches, armies and other organizations are also subject to similar crises.

Gouldner, for instance, studied a succession crisis in a gypsum plant in which the beloved, paternalistic head was replaced by a bureaucratically oriented executive. The new head was concerned with stricter enforcement of company rules. For instance, contrary to previous practice, he insisted on rigid observance of the "no absenteeism" rule; he attempted to end the workers' use of company property for their own purposes (e.g., home repairs); he increased the number of paper reports required of first-line supervisors. These innovations were resisted by workers and supervisors alike and resulted in the replacement of some of the more resistant personnel.[2]

Even fairly limited differences between a successor and his predecessor are believed to be a source of difficulties:

> Inquiry revealed that the woman, Miss A., was disliked because of an alleged lack of interest in the people with whom she worked. But analysis of these feelings led to the discovery that Miss B., the supervisor whom Miss A. was now about to succeed, had on every Monday morning summoned each girl to her office with the query "Have you any personal problems?" The workers' dislike of Miss A. then took on a different coloring. And it was finally discovered that their real antipathy toward her stemmed from the fact that, in contrast to Miss B., she discouraged the use of business time for the discussion of inconsequential personal matters.[3]

Levenson extended the point to all organizational positions by pointing out that some of the same elements of the succession crisis appear even when the person replaced is just a department head or division head. This can be interpreted as showing, in line with our earlier comments, that these positions are also endowed with some charisma.[4]

The succession crisis should not be viewed as a mere loss of organizational effectiveness, a crisis from which the organization has to recover. Actually the succession period is often the stage at which needed innovations are introduced to counteract earlier deterioration of the organization or to ward off challenges it faces during the succession period.

Some Critical Observations

In a critical examination of Weber's model elsewhere[5] we pointed out that: (a) Genuine charismatic leaders emerge within the established "head" positions; they re-endow the organization with legitimacy, so that their reign increases rather than depreciates its stock. In other words, a society or an organization might be rejuvenated without being disbanded. For example, the most distinguished American universities have known periods of deterioration following the deaths of their original founders, but very few have been disbanded and many have at a later state been revived by another charismatic leader who has restored their prominence. (b) The sharp distinction among the three modes of authority and social structure is exaggerated. Indeed there are many "mixed" types. For instance there were semi-traditional, semi-bureaucratic organizations in ancient Egypt,

[2] Alvin W. Gouldner, *Patterns of Industrial Bureaucracy* (Glencoe, Ill.: The Free Press, 1954).

[3] Edward C. Bursk (ed.), *Human Relations for Management* (New York: Harper, 1956), pp. 56–57.

[4] Bernard Levenson, "Bureaucratic Succession," in Amitai Etzioni (ed.), *Complex Organizations: A Sociological Reader* (New York: Holt, Rinehart and Winston, 1961), pp. 362–375.

[5] Amitai Etzioni, A *Comparative Analysis of Complex Organizations* (New York: The Free Press of Glencoe, 1961), Chapters IX and X.

bureaucracies: structure and legitimation

Imperial China, and medieval Byzantium in which hierarchical structures and adherence to rules and regulations were combined with a fairly diffuse, totalistic status structure, such as seems to characterize modern totalitarian regimes. (c) An organization might shift from a more bureaucratic to a more charismatic structure, and then back to a more bureaucratic one. Peacetime armies are highly bureaucratic. In time of war, especially in combat, they lose many of their bureaucratic qualities. Rules and regulations are waived or disregarded; personal leadership counts more than formal power positions; oral communications replace many written ones; separation of private and organizational life is largely abolished. Although novelists like to draw on the strains these transitions cause, as a rule they are carried out rather smoothly. After the war, though not without crisis, the organization again shifts gears and returns to a bureaucratic structure. Labor unions have similarly shifted from bureaucratic relations in periods of "business-as-usual" to charismatic relations as the tensions mount on the eve of and during the "combat" period of collective bargaining and strike. (d) Furthermore, the appearance of leaders with charismatic qualities is not limited to the top organizational position. Lower-ranking combat officers, low-ranking priests, and professors in universities occasionally exhibit a great deal of personal charisma.

Having considered some of the antecedents and components of the Structuralist approach, we turn now to apply some of the Structuralist insights to an analysis of problems and strains inherent in organizations, and to an analysis of mechanisms used by organizations in handling these problems and strains. First, we focus on internal problems such as those raised by the need to motivate and control organizational participants, and those deriving from the organization's need to create or apply knowledge to maintain or increase its rationality. Then we turn to a limited discussion of the external relations of organizations to their clients and to other organizations.

organizational
control
and leadership

six

Nowhere is the strain between the organization's needs and the participant's needs—between effectiveness, efficiency, and satisfaction—more evident than in the area of organizational control.[1] In part, the two sets of needs support each other. An increase in the income of a corporation might allow it to increase the wages and salaries it pays; an increase in the prestige of a school might increase the prestige of the teachers who work there. To the degree that the two sets of needs are compatible, little control is necessary. The participants will tend to do what is best for the organization in order to gratify their own needs, and the organization in seeking to serve its needs will serve theirs. But such meshing of needs is never complete, and is usually quite incomplete. The corporation's profit might grow, but the wages not be increased. Hence deliberate efforts have to be made by the organization to reward those who conform to its regulations and orders and to penalize those who do not. Thus the success of an organization is largely dependent on its ability to maintain control of its participants.

All social units control their members, but the problem of control in organizations is especially acute. Organizations as social units that serve specific purposes are artificial social units. They are planned, deliberately structured; they constantly and self-consciously review their performances and restructure themselves accordingly. In this sense they are unlike natural

[1] Discussion in this and the following chapter draws on the author's A *Comparative Analysis of Complex Organizations* (New York: The Free Press of Glencoe, 1961).

social units, such as the family, ethnic groups, or community. The artificial quality of organizations, their high concern with performance, their tendency to be far more complex than natural units, all make informal control inadequate and reliance on identification with the job impossible. Most organizations most of the time cannot rely on most of their participants to internalize their obligations, to carry out their assignments voluntarily, without additional incentives. Hence, organizations require formally structured distribution of rewards and sanctions to support compliance with their norms, regulations, and orders.

To fulfill its control function the organization must distribute its rewards and sanctions according to performance so that those whose performance is in line with the organizational norms will be rewarded and those whose performance deviates from it will be penalized. The dispensation of part of the rewards by the organization without regard to performances is more common in the less modern parts of the country than in the more advanced ones, and in less developed than in more developed countries; it is one of the reasons why organizational control is less effective in the less developed countries.[2]

Classification
of Means of Control

The means of control applied by an organization can be classified into three analytical categories: physical, material, or symbolic. The use of a gun, a whip, or a lock is physical since it affects the body; the threat to use physical sanctions is viewed as physical because the effect on the subject is similar in kind, though not in intensity, to the actual use. Control based on application of physical means is ascribed as *coercive power*.

Material rewards consist of goods and services. The granting of symbols (e.g., money) which allow one to acquire goods and services is classified as material because the effect on the recipient is similar to that of material means. The use of material means for control purposes constitutes *utilitarian power*.

Pure symbols are those whose use does not constitute a physical threat or a claim on material rewards. These include normative symbols, those of prestige and esteem; and social symbols, those of love and acceptance. When physical contact is used to symbolize love, or material objects to symbolize prestige, such contacts or objects are viewed as symbols because their effect on the recipient is similar to that of "pure" symbols. The use of symbols for control purposes is referred to as *normative, normative-social,* or *social power*. Normative power is exercised by those in higher ranks to control the lower ranks directly as when an officer gives a pep talk to his men. Normative-social power is used indirectly, as when the higher in rank appeals to the peer group of a subordinate to control him (e.g., as a teacher will call on a class to ignore the distractions of an exhibitionist child). Social power is the power which peers exercise over one another.

The use of various classes of means for control purposes—for power, in

[2] J. C. Abegglen, *The Japanese Factory: Aspects of Its Social Organization* (Glencoe, Ill.: The Free Press, 1958).

59

short—has different consequences in terms of the nature of the discipline elicited. All other things being equal, at least in most cultures, the use of coercive power is more alienating to those subject to it than is the use of utilitarian power, and the use of utilitarian power is more alienating than the use of normative power.[3] Or, to put it the other way around, normative power tends to generate more commitment than utilitarian, and utilitarian more than coercive. In other words, the application of symbolic means of control tends to convince people, that of material means tends to build up their self-oriented interests in conforming, and the use of physical means tends to force them to comply.

The powers organizations use differ largely according to the ranks of the participants that are controlled. Most organizations use less alienating means to control their higher rather than their lower ranks. For instance, coercive power—if used at all—is applied to lower participants; e.g., prisoners are put in solitary confinement if they try to escape. Higher participants, e.g., guards, are more often rewarded or sanctioned materially to insure their performances (e.g., tardiness is fined). In making comparative observations, it is hence essential to compare participants of the same rank in different kinds of organizations or different ranks within the same organization. If such pre caution is not observed, it is difficult to tell if the findings differ because of differences in rank or in the nature of the organizations, or both.

Comparing the controls applied to the lower ranks of different organizations is a fruitful way of classifying organizations, since differences in the nature of controls is indicative of and in this sense predicts many other differences among organizations. Most organizations most of the time use more than one kind of power. Control might be predominantly coercive, utilitarian, or normative. Among organizations in which the same mode of control predominates, there are still differences in the degree to which the predominant control is stressed. Ordering organizations from high to low according to the degree to which coercion is stressed, we find concentration camps, prisons, traditional correctional institutions, custodial mental hospitals, and prisoner-of-war camps. Ordering organizations from high to low according to the degree to which utilitarian power is predominant, we find blue-collar organizations such as factories, white-collar organizations such as insurance companies, banks, and the civil service, and peacetime military organizations. Normative power is predominant in religious organizations, ideological-political organizations, colleges and universities, voluntary associations, schools, and therapeutic mental hospitals.

Not every organizational type has one predominant pattern of control. Labor unions, for instance, fall into each of the three analytical categories. There are labor unions which rely heavily on coercive power to check deviant members, as in those unions that border on "underworld" organizations; there are "business-unions" in which control is largely built on the ability of the union representatives to "deliver the goods," i.e., to secure wage increases and other material improvements. Finally, there are unions in which control

---

[3] Unless specified otherwise, "normative power" is used to refer to both normative and normative-social power. Social power is not discussed because as such it is not an organizational power.

organizational control and leadership

is based on manipulation of ideological symbols, such as commitment to a Socialist ideology ("Those who do not pay their dues retard the service of the union to the cause of the laboring classes"), or in which the community of workers is recruited to exert informal pressures on members to follow the norms and orders of the organization ("strike-breakers are poor friends"). More complicated combinations need not be discussed here.[4]

The response of the participants to a particular use of power or combination of powers is determined not only by that use of power but also by the participants' social and cultural personalities. For instance, the same exercise of coercive power—a foreman slapping a worker—would elicit a more alienated response in working-class persons than it would in persons on "Skid Row"; in contemporary Britain than the Britain of three generations ago; in France than on the Ivory Coast; in an aggressive than in a subservient person. When, however, the effect of all these factors is "checked," when the effect of various means of control on the same group of workers is compared, the more normative the means of control used, the less alienating the exercise of power, and the more coercive the means, the more alienating the use of power. Utilitarian power rarely elicits as alienating a response as coercive power, nor does it as a rule generate as much commitment as normative power. To state it more concretely, most factory workers rarely feel as alienated as prisoners or as committed as church members.

A central finding of the comparative analysis of organizations is that organizations which differ in the kinds of control they use, and in the alienation or commitment they elicit, also differ in their organizational structure in many significant respects. Foremost among these structural differences are those of the place and role of leadership.

Leadership
and Organizational Control

The power of an organization to control its members rests either in specific positions (department head), a person (a persuasive man), or a combination of both (a persuasive department head). Personal power is always normative power; it is based on the manipulation of symbols and it serves to generate commitment to the person who commands it. Positional power, on the other hand, may be normative, coercive, or utilitarian. An individual whose power is chiefly derived from his organizational position is referred to as an *official*. An individual whose ability to control others is chiefly personal is referred to as an *informal leader*. One who commands both positional and personal power is a *formal leader*.

A person who is a leader in one field is not necessarily a leader in another; the football captain is not necessarily the politically most influential student. If we say that X is a leader, we must also specify the field in which he leads. There are many ways to distinguish among various kinds of activities. Two main spheres of activity an organization might wish to control are distinguished here: instrumental and expressive. *Instrumental* activities deal with the input of means into the organization and their distribution within

---

[4] See Etzioni, *A Comparative Analysis of Complex Organizations,* Chap. 3.

it. Mining and production are usually instrumental. *Expressive* activities affect interpersonal relations within the organization and the establishment of and adherence to norms by organizational participants. Social parties, ceremonies, and pep talks are all expressive. Bales and his associates have shown in studies of experimental groups that each of the two sets of activities tends to develop its own control positions. These are segregated in that different individuals tend to occupy them.[5] This is partly because these positions require incompatible role orientations and psychological characteristics.[6] It is hence fruitful to distinguish between instrumental and expressive leaders according to the kinds of activity they lead.

In organizations which tend to use coercion extensively, and whose lower ranks tend to be extremely alienated, the traditional prison is a typical example, control of work for the organization and behavior within it tends to be divided between officials and informal leaders. The guards are officials since their power is derived mainly from their positions and is largely independent of their personal qualities. However, much of the power to control the inmates lies in the hands of influential inmate leaders who hold no organizational positions and rely largely on their personal influence, and hence are informal leaders. Although wardens, and to some degree guards, have some personal influence over inmates, such influence as a rule is minor; in this sense there is no significant formal leadership in typical prisons. The ability of the prison to control the inmates depends largely on the amount of coercive power its officials command (e.g., how many guards there are) and on the relations between prison officials and informal inmate leaders. McCleery studied a prison in which the informal inmate leaders supported "law and order" until prison officials, following a change in personnel, undermined the informal leadership by trying to build up their (the officials') personal power and leadership. This reduced the cooperation between the informal leaders and the officials and eventually triggered a riot—that is, the prison officials lost control.[7] There is considerable doubt whether the higher in rank can serve as leaders for the lower ranks in coercive organizations. Officials, it seems, must either reduce the coerciveness of the organization, or give up hope of effective formal leadership.

Expressive activities in the prison are controlled almost exclusively by inmate leaders who set and reinforce the norms concerning right and wrong. The inmate leaders, for instance, determine if and when it is proper to speak to a guard, which crimes are more or less prestigious (murderers rank higher than rapists), and so on. Similarly, social relations are almost solely determined by the inmates and their leaders: "Stool pigeons" are ostracized, guards and other prison personnel are excluded. Prison officials have little control over these norms and relations. This is one of the reasons why rehabilitation

---

[5] Robert F. Bales, "The Equilibrium Problem in Small Groups," in Talcott Parsons, Robert F. Bales, and E. A. Shils (eds.), *Working Papers in the Theory of Action* (Glencoe, Ill.: The Free Press, 1953), pp. 111–161.

[6] Robert F. Bales, "Task Status and Likeability as a Function of Talking and Listening in Decision-Making Groups," in L. D. White (ed.), *The State of the Social Sciences* (Chicago: University of Chicago Press, 1956), pp. 148–161.

[7] R. H. McCleery, *Policy Change in Prison Management* (East Lansing: Michigan State University Press, 1957).

organizational control and leadership

efforts and psychiatric work tend to be unsuccessful in traditional prisons as long as the basic coercive structure is not changed.

Instrumental activities in the prison, especially the distribution of food and work, are more given to control by the organization and its officials, but even in this realm, informal inmate leaders have a great deal of power. Food and other scarce items such as cigarettes, which are distributed by the prison, tend to be redistributed by the inmates to bring the distribution of worldly goods into line with their norms, to reward those high on the inmate normative scale and status structure, and to penalize those who are low on both. Similarly, the allocation of work in the prison is affected by pressures the inmates' leaders exert on the officials. Responding to such pressures is often the only way an official can maintain the inmate leader's cooperation, which in turn is often required to maintain efficient organizational control. Furthermore, the inmates' control of instrumental activities extends to the production and acquisition of illicit goods and to the planning and execution of escape attempts. The officials' main instrumental control is ecological: It involves keeping the inmates in the prison and assigning them to various sections and cells.

Other organizations which rely heavily on coercive control have leadership structures similar to the prison's. However, the less coercion used, the more influence over the inmates' behavior it achieves, and the greater the probability that some formal leadership (e.g., leadership by higher ranks) in organizational positions will develop.[8] In the Japanese Relocation camps in the United States during World War II for instance, there was relatively less coercion than in the average prison. Although most of the camp personnel were treated as "officials" whose directives are followed because of their impersonal coercive—and sometimes remunerative—power, two staff members (mainly the "people-minded" director) had a personal power that could be called leadership, though it was largely limited to the instrumental-administrative sphere.[9]

Correctional institutions in which juvenile delinquents are held tend on the average to be less coercive than prisons. The same holds for mental hospitals, even of the older type, which often are almost as coercive as prisons, but not quite. Moreover, under pressure of the spread of the humanist viewpoint in society, there is a trend to increase the professional staff and to reduce the degree and frequency of coercion used in all these organizations. While initially much of the professional work in these organizations may yield little because the inmates are too highly alienated to enter a productive relationship with the treatment staff, as the professional staff increases in number and reduces the coercive nature of these organizations by exchanging social rewards for physical punishments, the influence of the therapists over the inmate population gradually grows, though it never approaches that of leaders in highly normative organizations.

In organizations which rely predominantly on normative controls, there

[8] Though the fact that reducing coercion often requires reducing some security measures, there are limits to the degree this can be done.

[9] A. H. Leighton, *The Governing of Men: General Principles and Recommendations Based on an Experience in a Japanese Relocation Camp* (Princeton: Princeton University Press, 1945), pp. 226–241.

tend to be few "officials" and few informal leaders; formal leaders effectively control most of the organizational participants. To the degree that informal leaders arise, within a parish, for instance, the tendency is to recruit them and gain their loyalty and cooperation by giving them part-time organizational positions, let us say as members of a church board. Or, the informal leaders might break away to form their own religious organization. In any case, the tendency is for the informal leaders to lose this status within the given organization and for control to remain largely in the hands of the formal leaders. Fichter discusses the development of positions in the Catholic Church parish which are filled by its active lay leaders. They encompass athletic, welfare, and social activities, but are directly or indirectly controlled by the pastor.[10] More recently, in large Protestant churches, there has been an increasing professionalization of leadership, with some of the activities formerly run by laity being taken over by paid workers. They are hired for religious education, counseling, recreational leadership, social work, and music, under the supervision of the ministers.[11]

Control in normative organizations is much more dependent on personal qualities than it is in coercive organizations. Hence, through various selection and socialization processes, normative organizations endeavor to staff the organizational positions from which control is exercised with individuals who command personal influence and thus combine positional normative power (e.g., the status of priest) with personal power (e.g., persuasive personality), that is, with formal leaders. Individuals lacking in personal power are often transferred to organizational positions in which no control is exercised, such as clerical or intellectual work. Such systematic efforts of normative organizations to provide leadership in formal positions, and the fairly high degree of success of such efforts, makes the evolution of informal leaders less likely.

Formal leaders in normative organizations are successful in exercising both instrumental and expressive control, although they are more concerned with controlling expressive activities. Some religious organizations provide offices for both kinds of leadership. Expressive matters tend to be the main functions of the major line of priests and bishops, instrumental activities the main functions of secondary positions such as deacons. In other religious organizations, control of instrumental activities is left largely to the laity while the organizations endeavor to maintain a monopoly of control over expressive matters—such as which prayers are to be said—in demanding adherence to the norms advocated by the church. Complete separation of the control of the two kinds of activities is impossible since instrumental matters (e.g., financing) affect expressive ones (e.g., the quality of Sunday or parochial schools), and vice versa. To insure the superiority of expressive matters, which are more directly related to the religious goals, over instrumental ones, and to counter tendencies toward goal displacement, religious organizations

---

[10] J. H. Fichter, *Social Relations in the Urban Parish* (Chicago: University of Chicago Press, 1954), pp. 3–49.

[11] P. M. Harrison, "Churches and the Laity Among Protestants," *Annals of the American Academy of Political and Social Science* (1960), 332:37–49.

organizational control and leadership

tend to insist on the superiority of the expressive leader over the instrumental one, whether the latter is an informal or a formal leader.

Just as prisons are typical coercive organizations, so religious organizations are typical normative organizations. The leadership structure of other highly normative organizations (e.g., the Communist party in Western societies) is quite similar to that of religious organizations.[12] Leadership is highly concentrated in organizational positions, such as the party secretary, and informal leaders are either given a position or expelled. Hospitals are normative organizations too, in that the doctor has to convince the patient to follow his advice. When it comes to assessing professional competence, the layman has little basis for rational judgment, and must go on other things. It is for this reason that the ability of the physician to make personal contact with the patient is an important one. Peterson, Andrews, Spain, and Greenberg state ". . . there is no linear correlation between the quality of medical care provided by a physician and his net income. Actually, this is hardly surprising in view of the fact that the lay public has few valid criteria for assessing a physician's competence. Indeed, it is part of folklore that a layman values a physician's personality or 'bedside manner' more highly than his profesional knowledge which may be less tangible or evident."[13] Hence the emphasis on personal qualities of leadership frequently starts with selection and socialization as far back as medical school. Although competence is emphasized in the selection of medical students, they are also screened to see whether they have the potentials of a "doctor's personality," often described as the ability to "impose one's will on the patient." The relative weight of this factor is difficult to establish, but it seems to be underestimated more than overestimated. It is widely accepted that "personality" is more important for lawyers than doctors, but future doctors do not think so. Thielens shows that 40 per cent of the medical students he studied consider "pleasing personality" to be the second most important factor making for a good doctor; "high intelligence" was listed as the first factor by 73 per cent. Law students asked a parallel question about factors making for a good lawyer gave the attributes virtually identical weight: 73 per cent listed intelligence first and 44 per cent put "pleasing personality" second.[14]

Control in utilitarian organizations is more evenly divided among organizational officials, formal leaders, and informal leaders of the employees. Moreover, the main concern of these organizations is with instrumental control of matters such as production and efficiency, and not with control of relations and norms established by the workers, so long as these do not adversely affect the instrumental activities. The particular leadership pattern that evolves depends largely on the relative degree of alienation or commitment of the employees. In industries where the workers are extremely alienated, their informal leaders, whether "old hands" or union stewards, tend to control most of the expressive activities and a number of instrumental ones. In such

[12] Cf. Philip Selznick, *The Organizational Weapon* (New York: McGraw-Hill, 1952).

[13] O. L. Peterson, L. P. Andrews, R. S. Spain, and B. G. Greenberg, "An Analytical Study of North Carolina General Practice," *Journal of Medical Education* (1956), 31:130.

[14] W. Thielens, Jr., "Some Comparisons of Entrants to Medical and Law School," *Journal of Legal Education* (1958), 2:148.

factories the foreman and higher-ranking supervisors, even if they wish to participate, are excluded from worker social relations, and the workers set the the norms which determine what is considered a proper day's work, if and when it is proper to speak to a foreman, and so on. However, the factory usually determines at least what work is to be done and some of the specifications on how it is to be carried out. A case where the workers' group developed both an instrumental and expressive leader is reported by Roethlisberger and Dickson. The group is reported to have revealed ". . . general dissatisfaction or unrest. In some, this was expressed by demands for advancement or transfers; in others, by a complaint about their lot in being kept on the job. . . . I [the observer] then noticed that two of the workers in particular held rather privileged positions in the group and were looked up to by the rest of the members. On these two the group seemed to place considerable responsibility. Of A they said: 'He can handle the engineers, inspectors and the supervisors. . . .' In speaking of B they expressed admiration for his work habits and capacities."

Although the instrumental capacities of B were respected, his expressive functions were not emphasized: " 'So-and-so talked too much a while ago, and B shut him up.' All expressed appreciation of his willingness to help them. A, in his interviews, told of fights with supervisors and arguments with engineers and inspectors. 'I made several machines work after an expert from the East said an adjustment was impossible.' B told of helping other adjusters. He said that he threatened to punch one operator in the nose because he had let the supervisor know that he had finished early."

The observer summarized the situation: "The supervisory control which is set up by management to regulate and govern the workers exercises little authority except to see that they are supplied with work. It is apparent that the group is protected from without by A . . . and protected from within by one (B) capable of administering punishment for any violation of the group standards." [15] The workers thus informally provide the expressive leaders and some of the instrumental ones, but the factory tends to exert some formal leadership in instrumental matters. Notice, however, that when alienation becomes quite high, workers may gain control of much of the work process itself.

In factories where the workers are less alienated, and in white-collar organizations, the formal leadership exerts considerably more control, especially over instrumental activities. The work carried out and its allocation among the various workers is largely determined by the organizational staff. Moreover, some of the expressive control, though rarely much of it, is acquired by those in organizational power positions. The norms followed by lower participants are much closer to those of the higher ranks and social relations are not so sharply segregated. The Christmas party, after all, is typical not of the alienated factory, but of the less alienated business office. It is in factories where alienation is not high to begin with, and in other utilitarian organizations, that the organization is successful in its efforts to increase commitment and to control expressive activities of the employees through such mechanisms

---

[15] F. J. Roethlisberger, and W. J. Dickson, *Management and the Worker* (Cambridge: Harvard University Press, 1939), pp. 383–384.

organizational control and l

as personnel departments, social workers, and the participation of lower ranks in decision-making. The same techniques are often less effective, from an organizational viewpoint, in structures in which the participants are more alienated.

It should not be concluded that when the organization is low on formal leadership it cannot achieve its goals effectively. Coercive organizations are built on the assumption that the officials cannot attain any leadership over the inmates and hence are equipped to deal with them by other means; utilitarian organizations can function quite effectively with formal leadership of instrumental and some expressive activities; normative organizations seem to be the only type that requires considerable formal leadership for operation and even these might do well with formal control of expressive activities and only some of the instrumental ones. Finally, as the study of the prison showed, even when leadership is highly concentrated in the hands of the lower participants themselves, so long as the cooperation of these informal leaders can be gained and maintained by the prison staff, this type of organization might control the inmates effectively without any formal leadership.

Further discussion of this subject would require detailed description and analysis of the nature of each kind of organization and the forms the distribution of leadership takes within it. This cannot be done in the limits of space available, nor is it necessary. Once the basic principles have been understood, they can be readily applied to whatever organization one is studying or wishes to examine. First, the nature of power typically employed by the organization has to be determined: Is it coercive, normative, or utilitarian; and to what degree? Next, the typical orientation of the group of participants one observes has to be established. How alienated or committed are they? This might then be related to the place of leadership within the organizational power structure. Is its locus to be found in organizational positions (formal) or among lower participants who have no organizational power positions (informal)? Is the organizational leadership only instrumental, only expressive, or both?

organizational
control and
other correlates

seven

The aim of organizational control is to ensure that rules are obeyed and orders followed. If an organization could recruit individuals who would conform on their own, or could educate its members so that they would conform without supervision, then there would be no need for control. Although this is never the case, there are very broad differences in the amount of control needed in organizations because of differences in recruitment and socialization of personnel.

Control, Selection, and Socialization

The role of recruitment, or selection, should be especially emphasized; the liberal-humanist tradition which prevails in the social sciences tends to underplay its importance and to stress that of socialization. Actually, various studies indicate that a small increase in the selectivity of an organization often results in a disproportionately large decrease in the investments required for control.[1] One reason is that a high percentage of the deviant acts are committed by a small percentage of the participants; hence, if these participants are screened out, the need for control declines sharply. According to one large-scale study, 95 per cent of the instances in which sanctions were applied in order to discipline students involved fewer than 5 per cent of the students.[2] If public schools were to screen out these students, con-

[1] K. J. Scudder, "The Open Institution," *Annals of the American Academy of Political and Social Science* (1954), 293:80–82.
[2] L. E. Vredevoe, A *Study of Practices in School Discipline*, mimeo, n.d.

trol problems could be expected to diminish (though not by as much as 95 per cent because it might not be easy to identify all potential and actual "trouble-makers").

Thus, the degree to which an organization selects its participants affects its control needs in terms of the amount of resources and effort it must invest to maintain the level of control considered adequate in view of its goal. This degree of selection varies among the three types of organizations. Coercive organizations are the least selective, accepting virtually everyone sent by such external agencies as the courts and the police. Notice, however, that when efforts are made to reduce coercion and to increase the use of other means of control—as when a rehabilitation program is tried in a prison, or a therapy program is launched in a custodial mental hospital—attempts are made to screen out the "toughest" inmates, to increase and improve the selection of new ones, and to re-select continuously the participants in a particular "open" ward. This has another interesting side effect: it maintains the appearance of an organization which relies highly on normative control while actually it relies indirectly on coercive control. Thus, for instance, youthful prisoners in upstate New York are allowed to work on a farm without bars or fences, but they know if they run away they are likely to be caught and sentenced to a longer period in a "closed" prison. Mental patients in "open" wards are often aware of the fact that if they "cause trouble" they will be locked in the "closed" ward. The excellent rehabilitation achievements of the California Institute for Men are in part, perhaps even mainly, the result of the better methods of treatment used there. But treatment and its results could hardly be unaffected, at least to some degree, by the fact that the inmates initially committed to this prison were selected from a large number of prisons, with a view to their potential ability to respond to such a minimum security program.[3]

Unlike typical coercive organizations, typical utilitarian organizations are highly selective. They often employ formal mechanisms—e.g., examinations, psychological tests, probation periods—to improve the selection of participants. All other things being equal, the higher the rank of the participant, the more carefully he is recruited and the less he is controlled once selected.

Finally, normative organizations vary primarily in their degree of selectivity. Some are extremely selective—most religious sects, for instance. Other religious organizations (e.g., the Roman Catholic Church) are highly unselective. The Soviet Communist party is highly selective; most democratic political parties in the West are highly unselective. Private schools are far more selective than public schools. In general, the more selective organizations are more effective and induce a deeper commitment from their participants than do organizations of lower selectivity. It should be pointed out, however, that these differences in effectiveness and commitment are only partial consequences of higher selectivity; in part they are due to other factors which tend to be associated with selectivity; but are not results of it. Highly selective organizations are generally richer and hence have more facilities available for achieving their goals. Highly selective schools, colleges, and hospitals,

[3] Scudder, *Annals of the American Academy of Political and Social Science*, 293: 80–82.

often set social and professional norms that are used to evaluate the effectiveness of the whole category of organizations to which they belong, though these norms—for instance, those of integrity required by the honor system—fit them much better than other organizations of the same category. Still it seems that even if all these other factors were controlled, highly selective normative organizations would still be more effective and generate stronger commitment than the less selective ones.

Selection is based on the qualities of participants as they enter the organization; organizational socialization subsequently adapts these qualities to make them similar to those required for satisfactory performance of organizational roles. As Simon points out, the more effective the socialization, the less the need for control.[4] On the other hand, socialization is itself affected by the means of control used, since some kinds of control more than others create a relationship between higher and lower ranks that is conducive to effective socialization. That the socialization efforts of coercive organizations are usually frustrated is reflected in the limited success of their therapeutic or rehabilitation programs. Organizations which rely heavily on normative power are the most successful in terms of their socialization achievements. Modern schools are a prime example. Utilitarian organizations tend to delegate socialization to other organizations, such as vocational schools and universities, and prefer careful selection of socialized persons to socialization by the organization. This raises the important point that socialization and selection can partially substitute for each other; i.e., the same level of control can be maintained by high selectivity and a low level of organizational socialization as with low selectivity and a high level of organizational socialization. (Of course, the amount of control needed is lower when selectivity and socialization are both high.)

For instance, although they are not necessarily aware of this, medical schools "fulfill" many of the premedical education requirements by selecting students who are relatives of professionals (especially doctors), which means that medical schools receive students who are already partially socialized; i.e., they have been introduced to many of the professional norms. Out of one sample of 498 medical students, 50 per cent had a relative who was a doctor, and 17 per cent had a doctor as a parent.[5] A study of medical students showed that there was little change in their basic normative orientation during their stay in medical school, when it could be expected that they would have undergone considerable socialization.[6] Thus the process of selection leaves medical schools with a smaller job of socializing students to their professional norms.

Control, Pervasiveness, and Scope

Means of control are used in all organizations to enforce the norms which set the standards of performance, but organizations differ markedly in the pervasiveness of the norms they attempt to set and en-

[4] H. A. Simon, *Administrative Behavior*, 2nd ed. (New York: Macmillan, 1957).
[5] W. Thielens, Jr., "Some Comparisons of Entrants to Medical and Law School," *Journal of Legal Education* (1958), 2:156.
[6] R. K. Merton, G. G. Reader, and Patricia L. Kendall, *The Student Physician* (Cambridge: Harvard University Press, 1957).

force. Some organizations (prisons, for instance), have a limited pervasiveness; they attempt to control only some of the activities carried out in the organization. Actually, the prison is more pervaded than pervasive; that is, many of the norms affecting inmate behavior have been set and are enforced by outside social units, such as the communities from which the inmates come. Other organizations (e.g., hospitals) are highly pervasive; they attempt to control most of the activities that take place within them, but few of those carried on outside. Still other organizations (e.g., churches) attempt to set and enforce norms both for activities which are carried on when the participants are on the premises of the organization and when they are not. These organizations pervade other social units.

In general, the more pervasive an organization is, the greater the efforts required to maintain effective control. Highly pervasive organizations, especially those that set norms for activities carried on outside the organization, almost inevitably have to stress normative control over their extra-organizational behavior. Low pervasiveness, on the other hand, can be enforced by any of the three types of means or combinations thereof, especially if the norms enforced are those which require mainly visible conformity (e.g., attendance), and little "invisible" conformity (e.g., sense of responsibility).

A factor which is substantively related to but analytically distinct from pervasiveness is organizational scope, which is determined by the number of activities carried out jointly by the participants in a particular organization. In organizations whose scope is narrow, participants share only one or a few activities (for example, social activities). Participants in organizations whose scope is broad share several kinds of activities, as in labor unions that carry on social and cultural activities as well as collective bargaining. Total organizations are those in which maximum scope is attained, as in convents.[7]

According to Goffman,

> The central feature of total institutions can be described as a breakdown of the barriers ordinarily separating these three spheres of life. First, all aspects of life are conducted in the same place and under the same single authority. Second, each phase of the member's daily activity is carried on in the immediate company of a large number of others, all of whom are treated alike and required to do the same thing together. Third, all phases of the day's activities are tightly scheduled, with one activity leading at a prearranged time into the next, and the whole sequence of activities being imposed from above through a system of explicit formal rulings and by a body of officials.[8]

There is no one-to-one relationship between scope and pervasiveness: An organization might set norms for more kinds of activities than are carried out jointly by participants, as the Communist party often does, or it might set norms for fewer activities than the joint ones, as in an army.

[7] For some insight into life in this type of organization, see Monica Baldwin, *I Leap over the Wall* (New York: Signet, 1957).
[8] Erving Goffman, "On the Characteristics of Total Institutions: the Inmate World," in Donald R. Cressey (ed.), *The Prison, Studies in Institutional Organization and Change* (New York: Holt, Rinehart and Winston, 1961), p. 17.

71

High scope enhances normative control, is a necessary condition of coercive control, and seems to affect utilitarian control negatively. High scope enhances normative control because it separates the participants from social groups other than the organization and tends to increase their involvement in it. A comparison of commuter and residential colleges illustrates this point. In commuter colleges some of the educational impact is not attained and some is countered, since the students' involvement in the college as a social unit is limited, and since they have significant and active social ties to external groups, \ hich often support different norms. All other things being equal, residential colleges can have a considerably deeper educational impact, with the same investment in normative control. (Education is here considered in its broadest sense and includes character development and not just communication of skills and information.) The value of high scope for educational purposes is fully recognized by this study of a military academy:

> This clean break with the past must be achieved in a relatively short period. For two months, therefore, the swab is not allowed to leave the base or to engage in social intercourse with non-cadets. This complete isolation helps to produce a unified group of swabs, rather than a heterogeneous collection of persons of high and low status. Uniforms are issued on the first day, and discussions of wealth and family background are taboo. Although the pay of the cadet is very low, he is not permitted to receive money from home. The role of cadet must supersede other roles the individual has been accustomed to play. There are few clues left which will reveal social status in the outside world.[9]

In the past, the utilitarian organizations often attempted to maintain a broad scope, as in the company town; and then more recently, corporations were advised to provide their workers with educational, recreational, and residential facilities. However, in the last decade, the tendency has been for corporations to reduce their scope in these areas without loss and probably with some gain in the effectiveness of their control structures.[10] Cafeteria service is more often provided by an outsider than by the organization; the workers are now less frequently encouraged to bowl as a factory team; and business organizations attempt less often to counsel their employees on personal problems. In cases where the organization did not take the initiative to reduce scope, the employees often did, as the following case illustrates:

> After 15 years as a company town servicing the big-secret plutonium works known as the Hanford Atomic Project, Richland had voted itself out from the paternalistic wings of the Atomic Energy Commission and General Electric, prime AEC contractor. . . . No family could own its home. Not general necessity but General Electric determined the site of stores and set their rents. Police, firemen, even the city librarian were G.E. employees. More and more, Richland residents began to move out to nearby Pasco and

[9] Sanford M. Dornbusch, "The Military Academy as an Assimilating Institution," *Social Forces* (1955), 33:317.

[10] R. Likert, "Implication of Organizational Research," *First Management Work Conference in Developing Human Resources* (Washington, D.C.: National Training Laboratories, 1956); J. F. Scott and R. P. Lynton, *The Community Factor in Modern Technology* (Paris: UNESCO, 1952), pp. 60, 77–78.

organizational control and other correlates

Kenneswick, to own their homes and chat over the fence with non-G.E. neighbors. . . . In 1955 a petition for incorporation as an independent municipality lost 3 to 1. . . . After another petition for incorporation was circulated, Richlanders poured out last July [1958] to approve it, 5 to 1.[11]

The citizens of modern societies are socialized to shift constantly among various social units such as the family, the community, and the work unit. The relatively high separation and low scope of all these units allows the typically modern mode of managing tension to operate. Tensions generated in one unit are released in another by changing partners, thus "localizing" rather than "totalizing" conflicts, and by shifting back and forth between social units in which rational, efficient behavior is demanded (a form of behavior which is particularly taxing) and those in which the norm is non-rational behavior (which is comparatively relaxing). Those utilitarian organizations which have a high scope, which fuse work and non-work units, prevent both the localization of conflict and the shift of participants to units relatively free of rational considerations. This might explain the reduction in tensions resulting from the recent tendency to separate more fully work and non-work units.

Coercive organizations must maintain total scope, for unless the participants carry out all their activities within the one organization, they would have too many opportunities to escape. Moreover, the deprivational character of total scope, of separating the inmates from all non-organizational units, is used as a major means of punishment and hence of control. (For instance, a prisoner who has violated the prison's rules may find his sentence extended.) Attempts to reduce the use of coercion and to rely more on normative power, as when rehabilitation or therapeutic programs are introduced, are frequently associated with efforts to reduce scope by allowing more visits by outsiders, initiating programs of work outside the prison, allowing mental patients to spend week ends or the night at home, and the like.

Further Research

The study of control along the lines suggested in the last two chapters is still in its beginning. It will have to be extended in many directions before we can understand adequately the factors that affect control and are affected by it. Especially novel, and hence in need of verification, are statements that are comparative, as are the various ideas presented above on the differences among coercive, utilitarian, and normative organizations. For the research-minded reader, we indicate some directions investigation in this area might take, apart from testing the validity of earlier statements.

Among the many factors which affect organizational control, and about which we have little systematic knowledge, the organizational environment looms large. To use coercion, an organization needs social license. The state is jealous of its coercive power and is reluctant to delegate it. Moreover, such a license, when granted, usually sets an upper limit on the coercion to be used (mental hospitals can lock patients up, but cannot legitimately whip them) and specifies the conditions under which coercion can be exercised

[11] *Time*, December 22, 1958, p. 18.

(prisons cannot hang trouble-makers). Utilitarian controls are affected by the market position of the organization under study, and by the general state of the market. Depressions and inflations also affect the ability of an organization to use utilitarian power, though some voluntary associations succeed in increasing their income and assets while those of the members decline.[12]

The environmental conditions affecting an organization's normative power are less clear. The presence or absence of competitive organizations seems to be important here; the normative power of a church seems to be higher in countries in which it represents the sole religion than in countries where it must compete with other religions and secular ideologies.

The effect of the environment on an organization is in part determined by the nature of the organization; that is, the same environment has more effect on some (e.g., "weak" organizations) than on others. Legislatures and politicians have more effect on public than private colleges, and on Protestant than on Catholic colleges. The effect of the community seems to vary less from one college type to another, whereas alumni seem to affect more larger than smaller colleges. It is not our purpose here to explore the significance of these specific differences but rather to emphasize that the same environment has different effects on different types of organization. (The particular differential effects here are of course due in part to some difference in the environment hidden behind the seemingly identical categories of "community," "politicians," etc.)

We know little about the effect of organizational environment on control even in Western societies. The study of this relationship in other cultures, especially in less developed and non-democratic societies, remains one of the major tasks of social scientists. Similarly, we know much more about control of low-ranking participants than of high-ranking ones, and clearly the control of the higher ranks is at least as important. Finally, we need to know more about the dynamics of control. How do changes in leadership affect changes in the level of alienation? What kinds of leadership emerge as alienation changes? Does reduction in scope always support normative control? What are the limits of effective socialization as a means of minimizing control and maximizing commitment, of increasing by the same effort both organizational effectiveness and satisfaction of the participants?

[12] John E. Tsonderos, "Organizational Change in Terms of a Series of Selected Variables," *American Sociological Review* (1955), 20:206–210.

organizational control and other correlates

administrative
and professional
authority

eight

The ultimate source of the organizational dilemmas reviewed up to this point is the incomplete matching of the personalities of the participants with their organizational roles. If personalities could be shaped to fit specific organizational roles, or organizational roles to fit specific personalities, many of the pressures to displace goals, much of the need to control performance, and a good part of the alienation would disappear. Such matching is, of course, as likely as an economy without scarcity and hence without prices. But even if all the dilemmas which result from the incomplete articulation of personality and organization were resolved, there still would remain those which are consequences of conflicting tendencies built into the organizational structure.

Probably the most important structural dilemma is the inevitable strain imposed on the organization by the use of knowledge. All social units use knowledge, but organizations use more knowledge more systematically than do other social units. Moreover, most knowledge is created in organizations and passed from generation to generation—i.e., preserved—by organizations. It is here that Weber overlooked one necessary distinction: He viewed bureaucratic or administrative authority as based on technical knowledge or training; the subordinates, he thought, accept rules and orders as legitimate because they consider being rational being right, and regard their superiors more rational.[1] One is not "stretching" Weber much to suggest that he

[1] Max Weber (Talcott Parsons, ed.; A. M. Henderson and Talcott Parsons, trans.), *The Theory of Social and Economic Organization* (New York: Oxford University Press, 1947), p. 339

thought that the higher the rank of an official the better equipped he tends to be either in terms of formal education (e.g., academic degrees) or in terms of merit and experience. Examinations and promotion according to merit, Weber pointed out, help to establish such association between rank and knowledge. To a degree, this conception is valid. There is considerable evidence that persons who have only a high-school education will be more frequently found in lower ranks, and college-educated persons in the higher ones. There is probably some correlation between IQ and rank, in the sense that on the average the IQ of the top third of an organization is likely to be higher than that of the lowest third. One could argue that when the superiority-of-knowledge requirement is not fulfilled, when the higher in rank knows less or has a lower IQ than the lower in rank, his orders might still be followed because of his power to enforce them; but Weber would counter that such orders would not be considered legitimate and hence the official would have power but not authority.

Still the reader is correct in his intuition that there is something fundamentally wrong with the notion of viewing the bureaucracy as a hierarchy in which the more rational rule the less rational. There are two reasons. First, by far most of the trained members of the organization are found not in the highest but in the middle ranks, and not in the regular line or command positions but around them. Depending on the type of organization, they are referred to as experts, staff, professionals, specialists, or by the names of their respective professions. Second, the most basic principle of administrative authority and the most basic principle of authority based on knowledge— or professional authority—not only are not identical but are quite incompatible.

Administrative vs. Professional Authority

Administration assumes a power hierarchy. Without a clear ordering of higher and lower in rank, in which the higher in rank have more power than the lower ones and hence can control and coordinate the latter's activities, the basic principle of administration is violated; the organization ceases to be a coordinated tool. However, knowledge is largely an individual property; unlike other organization means, it cannot be transferred from one person to another by decree. Creativity is basically individual and can only to a very limited degree be ordered and coordinated by the superior in rank. Even the application of knowledge is basically an individual act, at least in the sense that the individual professional has the ultimate responsibility for his professional decision. The surgeon has to decide whether or not to operate. Students of the professions have pointed out that the autonomy granted to professionals who are basically responsible to their consciences (though they may be censured by their peers and in extreme cases by the courts) is necessary for effective professional work. Only if immune from ordinary social pressures and free to innovate, to experiment, to take risks without the usual social repercussions of failure, can a professional carry out his work effectively. It is this highly individualized principle which is diametrically opposed to the very essence of the organizational principle of control and coordination by superiors—i.e., the principle of

76

administrative authority. In other words, the ultimate justification for a professional act is that it is, to the best of the professional's knowledge, the right act. He might consult his colleagues before he acts, but the decision is his. If he errs, he still will be defended by his peers. The ultimate justification of an administrative act, however, is that it is in line with the organization's rules and regulations, and that it has been approved—directly or by implication—by a superior rank.

The Organization of Knowledge

The question is how to create and use knowledge without undermining the organization. Some knowledge is formulated and applied in strictly private situations. In the traditional professions, medicine and law, much work is carried out in non-organizational contexts—in face-to-face interaction with clients. But as the need for costly resources and auxiliary staff has grown, even the traditional professions face mounting pressures to transfer their work to organizational structures such as the hospital and the law firm. Similarly, while most artistic work is still conducted in private contexts, often in specially segregated sectors of society in which an individual's autonomy is particularly high, much of the cognitive creativity, particularly in scientific research, has become embedded in organizational structures for reasons similar to those in medicine and law.

In addition there are several professions in which the amount of knowledge (as measured in years of training) and the degree of personal responsibility (as measured in the degree to which privileged communications—which the recipient is bound not to divulge—or questions of life and death are involved) are lower than in the older or highly creative, cognitive professions. Engineering and nursing are cases in point. These professions can be more easily integrated into organizational structures than can medicine or law, for example. Most professional work at this level is carried out within organizations rather than in private practice, and it is more given to supervision by persons higher in rank (who have more administrative authority but no more, or even less, professional competence) than the work of the professions discussed above.

To some degree, organizations circumvent the problem of knowledge by "buying" it from the outside, as when a corporation contracts for a market study from a research organization; i.e., it specifies the type of knowledge it needs and it agrees with the research group on price, but then it largely withdraws from control over the professional work. There are, however, sharp limitations on the extent to which knowledge can be recruited in this way, particularly since organizations consume such large amounts of knowledge and they tend to need more reliable control on its nature and flow. There are three basic ways in which knowledge is handled within organizations:

1. Knowledge is produced, applied, preserved, or communicated in organizations especially established for these purposes. These are *professional organizations*, which are characterized not only by the goals they pursue but also by the high proportion of professionals on their staff (at least 50 per cent) and by the authority relations between professionals and non-

77

professionals which are so structured that professionals have superior authority over the major goal activities of the organization, a point which is explored below. Professional organizations include universities, colleges, most schools, research organizations, therapeutic mental hospitals, the larger general hospitals, and social-work agencies. For certain purposes it is useful to distinguish between those organizations employing professionals whose professional training is long (5 years or more), and those employing professionals whose training is shorter (less than 5 years). The former we call *full-fledged professional* organizations; the latter, *semi-professional* organizations. Generally associated with differences in training of the professionals in these two types of organizations are differences in goals, in privileges, and in concern with matters of life and death. "Pure" professional organizations are primarily devoted to the creation and application of knowledge; their professionals are usually protected in their work by the guarantee of privileged communication, and they are often concerned with matters of life and death. Semi-professional organizations are more concerned with the communication and, to a lesser extent, the application of knowledge, their professionals are less likely to be guaranteed the right of privileged communications, and they are rarely directly concerned with matters of life and death.

2. There are *service organizations* in which professionals are provided with the instruments, facilities, and auxiliary staff required for their work. The professionals however are not employed by the organization nor subordinated to its administrators.

3. Professionals may be employed by organizations whose goals are *non-professional*, such as industrial and military establishments. Here professionals are often assigned to special divisions or positions, which to one degree or another take into account their special needs.

We shall first discuss the relation between the two authority principles—that of knowledge and that of administration—in non-professional organizations, then in "full-fledged" professional organizations, in semi-professional organizations, and finally in service organizations.

Professional Authority
in Non-professional Organizations

Superiority of Administrative Authority

By far the largest and most common non-professional organizations are the production organizations which are privately owned and managed. The organizational goal of private business is to make profits. The major means are production and exchange. While professionals deal with various aspects of the production and exchange process—that is, with means such as engineering, quality control, and marketing—the manager (the corporation's equivalent of the administrator) is expected to coordinate the various activities in such a way that the major organizational goal—profit-making—will be maximized. This seems to be one of the reasons why modern corporations prefer to have as top executives people with administrative experience rather than professionals. (In a study of the occupational backgrounds of the chief executives of American industry in 1950, admin-

administrative and professional authority

istration was found to have been the principal occupation of 43.1 per cent, 11.8 per cent were defined as entrepreneurs; finance had been the field of 12.4 per cent; and only 12.6 per cent had been engineers.[2] People with scientific backgrounds such as research workers are even less likely to become heads of private business. Only about 4 per cent of the presidents of American corporations had such a background.[3])

In general, the goals of private business are consistent with administrative orientations. The economic orientation of the organization and the bureaucratic orientation of the administrative role share an orientation toward rational combination of means and development of rational procedures to maximize goals which are considered as given. The social and cultural conditions that support modern economic activities also support modern administration (see below, Ch. 10). Professional and economic orientations are less compatible.

When people with strong professional orientations take over managerial roles, a conflict between the organizational goals and the professional orientation usually occurs. Homans reports an interesting case in which the influence of professionally oriented participants was greater than in most corporations.[4] He discusses an electrical equipment company which was owned, managed, and staffed by engineers. Management, which was in the hands of administration-oriented engineers, suffered from pressure to pursue uneconomic goals by the professionally oriented design engineers. The design engineers were charged with being indifferent to the "general welfare of the company"—that is, to profit-making—as "shown by their lack of concern with finance, sales, and the practical needs of the consumer and by their habit of spending months on an aspect of design that had only theoretical importance." This caused considerable tension between the managerial and professionally oriented groups, tension to which this company was especially sensitive because of its high dependence on professional work and the special structure of ownership. A power struggle resulted which ended with a clearer subordination of the design engineers (staff) to the managerial engineers (line). This was mandatory "if the company was to survive and increase its sales," as Homans put it. The treasurer (a non-professional in this context) became the most influential member of the new management. In short, in a corporation where the professionals exerted a strong influence, the existence of the organization was threatened, considerable internal tension was generated, and finally the organizational power structure was changed toward a more usual structure, with the professionally minded more clearly subordinated. In other words, the organizational authority structure was made more compatible with the goals of the organization. The orientations of the managers and the goals of private business seem to match. When a professional orientation dominates, this tends to "displace" the profit goal of privately owned economic organizations.

[2] M. Newcomer, *The Big Business Executive* (New York: Columbia University Press, 1955), p. 92.
[3] See G. H. Copeman, *Leaders of British Industry* (London: Gee and Co., 1955).
[4] George C. Homans, *The Human Group* (New York: Harcourt, Brace, 1950), pp. 369–414.

The way the two kinds of authority are combined in corporations and other non-professional organizations is often referred to as "staff and line." The managers, whose authority is administrative, direct the major goal activities; the professionals deal with knowledge as a means, and with the knowledge aspect of other means. They are in a subordinate position to the managers. Thus, in cases of conflict between the two criteria for decision-making, the organizational power structure is slanted in favor of the administrative authority. However, professional subordinates are treated differently from regular subordinates; they are not treated as are lower ranks in a line structure, but as "staff," a term which designates positions outside the regular chain of command or "line" and implies a certain amount of autonomy.

There are two interpretations of the relationship between staff and line. According to one approach, the staff has no administrative authority whatsoever. It advises the administrators (line authority) on what action to take. The staff does not issue orders to those lower in rank; if it desires any action or correction, this must be achieved through those in the line rank. According to the second approach, the staff, while advising the line on various issues, also takes responsibility for limited areas of activity.[5] That is, on some matters the staff directly issues orders to the lower participants.

Both combinations of the two authority principles generate considerable strain. In the first, where the line alone issues orders, the line tends to be overloaded by demands for decisions, and tends to repel at least some of the professional advice and requests for action of the staff. Line personnel have a large number of other functional requirements they must look after. They rarely comprehend fully the bases of actions requested by the staff, and they tend to neglect or at least to under-represent the staff demands. In the second approach the lower line is subordinated to two authorities at a time. There is a functional division of control between the two authorities, in the sense that professional matters are assigned to staff control and all the others to line control. In practice, while there are some matters that fall clearly into one category or the other, many issues can be viewed as either professional or administrative matters or both. This leads to the issuance of conflicting orders and gives the lower in rank the opportunity to play one authority against the other.

Dalton called attention to the tendencies of the higher- and lower-ranking line personnel to form a coalition against the staff personnel. He found the reason in the sociological differences that unite the line against the staff. The staff is generally younger and much more likely to be college-educated than the line, although the latter have greater organizational experience and hence resent advice and suggestions from the relatively inexperienced staff. Furthermore, the two groups are divided by differences in patterns of speech

[5] On the two approaches, see H. A. Simon, D. W. Smithburg, and V. A. Thompson, *Public Administration* (New York: Knopf, 1956), pp. 280–295; and A. W. Gouldner, *Patterns of Industrial Bureaucracy* (Glencoe, Ill.: The Free Press, 1954), pp. 224–228.

administrative and professional authority

and dress, recreational preferences, etc.[6] In these areas, the higher-ranking line is often closer to the lower-ranking line than to the staff. Thus the tensions between staff and line derive not only from the organizational conflicts resulting from overloading or lack of clear division of authority, but also from differences in sociological background. (These differences might decline as more and more higher line officials gain college education, or a new division might emerge between the A.B. and B.S. on the one hand, and the Ph.D.'s on the other.)

In spite of important differences between the two approaches, staff authority in both is subordinate to line authority and the line is identified with administrative authority and the staff with professional authority. While it is obvious that there are some staff functions which are not carried out by professionals, and that there are some professionals among the line personnel, there is a high correlation between staff and professionals, and between line and non-professionals.

In organizations whose goal is non-professional (e.g., profit-making), it is considered desirable for administrators to have the major (line) authority because they direct the major goal activity. Professionals deal only with means, with secondary activities. Therefore it is functional for the organization that they have no, or only limited (staff), authority, and they be ultimately subordinated to administrators. This generally is the case in corporations and armies.

Professionals
in Professional Organizations

In full-fledged professional organizations the staff-professional line-administrator correlation, insofar as such distinctions apply at all, is reversed. Although administrative authority is suitable for the major goal activities in private business, in professional organizations administrators are in charge of secondary activities; they administer *means* to the major activity carried out by professionals. In other words, to the extent that there is a staff-line relationship at all, professionals should hold the major authority and administrators the secondary staff authority. Administrators offer advice about the economic and organizational implications of various activities planned by the professionals. The final decision is, functionally speaking, in the hands of the various professionals and their decision-making bodies, such as committees and boards. The professor decides what research he is going to undertake and to a large degree what he is going to teach; the physician determines the treatment to be given to the patient.

Administrators may raise objections. They may point out that a certain drug is too expensive or that a certain teaching policy will decrease the number of students in a way that endangers the financing of a university. But functionally the professional is the one to decide on his discretion to what degree these administrative considerations should be taken into account.

---

[6] Melville Dalton, "Conflicts Between Staff and Line Managerial Officers," *American Sociological Review* (1950), 15:342–351.

It is interesting to note that some of the complaints usually made against professionals in non-professional organizations are made against administrators in professional organizations: They are said to lose sight of the major goal of the organization in pursuit of their specific limited responsibilities. Professionals in private business are sometimes criticized as being too committed to science, craftsmanship, and abstract ideas; administrators in professional organizations are deprecated because they are too committed to their specialties—"efficiency" and economy.

Many of the sociological differences between professionals and managers in private business are reversed in professional organizations. Professionals enter professional organizations younger and at lower positions (i.e., as students, research assistants, or interns) than managers do. The range of mobility of administrators is usually relatively limited, and a professional is more likely to reach the top position of institutional head.

In private business, overinfluence by professionals threatens the realization of organizational goals and sometimes even the organization's existence. In professional organizations overinfluence by the administration, which takes the form of ritualization of means, undermines the goals for which the organization has been established and endangers the conditions under which knowledge can be created and institutionalized (as, for instance, academic freedom).

Who Is Superior?

Heading a professional organization constitutes a special dilemma. It is a typical case of institutionalized role conflict.[7] On the one hand, the role should be in the hands of a professional in order to ensure that the commitments of the head will match organizational goals. A professional at the head of the authority structure will mean that professional activity is recognized as the major goal activity, and that the needs of professionals will be more likely to receive understanding attention. On the other hand, organizations have needs that are unrelated to their specific goal activity. Organizations have to obtain funds to finance their activities, recruit personnel to staff the various functions, and allocate the funds and personnel which have been recruited. Organizational heads must know how to keep the system integrated by giving the right amount of attention and funds to the various organizational needs, including secondary needs. A professional may endanger the integration of the professional organization by over-emphasizing the major goal activity and neglecting secondary functions. He may lack skill in human relations. In short, the role of head of professional organizations requires two incompatible sets of orientations, personal characteristics, and aptitudes. If the role is performed by either a lay administrator or a typical professional, one set of considerations is likely to be emphasized to the neglect of the other.

The severity of the dilemma is increased because of the motivational

---

[7] By *role* we mean the behavior expected from a person in the particular position. On this concept, see Melvin Seeman, "Role Conflict and Ambivalent Leadership," *American Sociological Review* (1953), 18:373–380.

administrative and professional authority

pattern of typical professionals. Most successful professionals are not motivated to become administrators. Some would refuse any administrative role, including the top one of university president or hospital chief, because of their commitment to professional values and ties to professional groups, and because they feel that they would not be capable of performing the administrative role successfully. Even those professionals who would not reject the distinguished and powerful role of organizational head avoid the administrative roles that are training grounds for and channels of mobility to these top positions. Thus many academicians refuse to become deans, not to mention associate or assistant deans, and try to avoid if possible the role of department chairman. Those who are willing to accept administrative roles are often less committed to professional values than their colleagues,[8] or view it as a transitional status, not a career. The same can be said about administrative appointments in hospitals. For instance, in the mental hospital studied by Stanton and Schwartz, the role of administrative psychiatrist is fulfilled at the beginning of the training period.[9] It is considered an undesirable chore that must be endured before turning to the real job. Psychiatrists who complete their training tend to withdraw to private practice. From other studies, especially those of state mental hospitals, it appears that those who stay are often less competent and less committed to professional values than those who leave.

The Professionally Oriented Administrator

There are various solutions to this dilemma. By far the most widespread one is the rule of the professionally oriented administrator. Such an administrator is one who combines a professional education with a managerial personality and practice. Goal as well as means activities seem to be handled best when such a person is the institutional head. Because of his training, he is more likely to understand the special needs of a professional organization and its staff than a lay administrator, and, because of his personal characteristics, he is more likely to be skilled in handling the needs and requests of his professional colleagues as well as those of the administrative staff.

There are two major sources of professionally oriented administrators. One is the professionals themselves. Some feel that they have little chance of becoming outstanding professionals in their field. Often the same people find that they are relatively more skilled in administrative activities. Thus they gravitate toward administrative jobs by serving on committees and by assuming minor administrative roles; some eventually become top administrators. Contrary to the popular belief, most university presidents are former professors. Wilson found that out of the 30 universities he studied, 28 had presidents who had been professors, albeit none a very eminent scholar.[10]

[8] A. W. Gouldner, "Cosmopolitans and Locals: Toward an Analysis of Latent Social Roles," *Administrative Science Quarterly* (1957), 2:281–306. For a more recent study, see Barney G. Glaser, "Attraction, Autonomy, and Reciprocity in the Scientist-Supervisor Relations," *Administrative Science Quarterly* (1963), 8:379–398.

[9] A. H. Stanton and M. S. Schwartz, *The Mental Hospital* (New York: Basic Books, 1954).

[10] L. Wilson, *The Academic Man* (New York: Oxford University Press, 1942), p. 85.

It seems that academicians who are inclined to take administrative jobs, or who are organization-oriented, not only publish less in quantity and quality after they have entered administrative positions but also tended to publish less before they accepted such jobs.

Of the heads of mental hospitals studied, 74.2 per cent are physicians.[11] Although there is no study on their professional eminence as compared to that of private practitioners, it seems that the heads of mental hospitals do not include the most successful psychiatrists. Only about 22 per cent of the heads of general hospitals are physicians.[12] Where these are full-time jobs, the statement made about the heads of mental hospitals seems to apply here also.

The second source of professionally-oriented administrators is special training. In recent years there has been a movement toward developing training programs for specialized administration, such as hospital administration and research administration. A considerable number of teachers, for example, return to universities to take courses in administrative education before they become school principals.

The advantages of specialized administrators over lay administrators are obvious. They are trained for their particular role and have considerable understanding of the organization in which they are about to function before they enter it. They are sensitized to the special tensions of working with professionals, and they share some of their professional values. On the other hand, they are less prepared for their role than the professionally oriented administrators from the first source who have a deeper commitment to professional values, command more professional respect, and have a greater number of social ties with professionals.

Although most professional organizations are controlled by professionals or professionally oriented administrators, some are controlled by lay administrators. By lay administrators we mean administrators who have no training in serving the major goal activities of the organization. This holds for 2 out of the 30 universities studied by Wilson, for fewer than 10 per cent of the schools, for 20.5 per cent of the mental hospitals, and for about 38 per cent of the general hospitals. (Wilson's study is small, the other data is based on large populations.)

The strain created by lay administrators in professional organizations leads to goal displacement. When the hierarchy of authority is in inverse relation to the hierarchy of goals and means, there is considerable danger that the goals will be subverted. Of course there are many other factors which may have such a distorting influence; but lay administrators are more likely to cause displacement than are other administrators.

The major function of mental hospitals is to cure the patient; however, mental hospitals are often custodial institutions which serve as places to keep the patients so that they will not endanger or disturb the public.[13]

[11] L. Block, "Ready Reference of Hospital Facts," *Hospital Topics* (1956), 34:23.
[12] *Ibid.*, pp. 121–136.
[13] See M. Greenblatt, R. H. York, and E. L. Brown with R. W. Hyde, *From Custodial to Therapeutic Patient Care in Mental Hospitals* (New York: Russell Sage Foundation, 1955); and M. Greenblatt, D. J. Levinson, and R. H. Williams (eds.), *The Patient and the Mental Hospital* (Glencoe, Ill.: The Free Press, 1957), especially p. 320.

administrative and professional authority

Although some custodial activities are an essential part of the means that the mental hospital has to apply in order to serve its therapeutic goal, there is a constant danger that these means will become a major focus of its activities. Thus a mental patient might be transferred from closed to open ward not when it is best for his recovery, but when it is most convenient for the staff, or when he is considered to constitute a lesser threat to the community should he escape.

A similar distortion of the relation between goals and means seems to occur in some vocational schools. These schools are established in order to train pupils in vocations which they will pursue in later years, but the predominant effort of these organizations is often directed to keeping teenagers off the street. As long as they fulfill this goal, little attention is paid to the quality of the teachers, the adequacy of the equipment, and the relation between the vocations which the school teaches and those which the market can absorb.

Universities constitute a more complicated case. Whereas in the two cases discussed above the legitimate goal is neglected and emphasis is put on means, here the dilemma is different: A secondary goal threatens to become the major goal. Although there is some controversy over what constitute the primary and the secondary goals of outstanding universities, it seems fair to conclude that a majority of the members of their professional staff would see research as primary and teaching as secondary. This is well-reflected in the the prestige and promotion systems.[14] But there is constant danger that the university will respond to pressures to give more money and attention to teaching and less to research.

There are many sources for these strains. To begin with, some goals seem to be more precarious than others. Professionals themselves may generate such pressures; for example, some physicians see in the hospital a research institution and try to refuse "uninteresting" cases. The community in the form of an alumni association, the chamber of commerce, and the board of trustees is another source of these pressures. But the head of the organization has a strategic position in this important institutional conflict. If he is in sympathy with the primary organizational goal, he can do much to neutralize the conflicting pressures and to mobilize the forces that support the primary goals. If he himself joins those who try to give priority to secondary goals, or who try to ritualize means or introduce illegitimate goals (as when, for instance, profit-making becomes the primary goal of a hospital), then organizational goals will be surely distorted. Professional organizations cater to goals which are usually upheld by the professional. Hence a lay administrator with a strong bureaucratic orientation seems to be more likely to endanger the professional goals than a professional or a professionally oriented administrator.

Center of Authority

Weber's bureaucratic theory assumes that there is one major structure of authority (the line). It may be very complicated and have many branches, but it always has one center of authority where final

14 See T. Caplow and R. J. McGee, *The Academic Marketplace* (New York: Basic Books, 1958).

85

decisions are made and conflicts can be resolved. The main authority line is directly related to the primary goal activity of the organization and only indirectly to secondary (means) activities.

In professional organizations there seems to be no line in this sense. It has been suggested that this means that professional organizations have a "functional" structure of authority. As Moore has pointed out, this concept is far from being clear.[15] It usually refers to the fact that low level persons are subordinated to two or more authorities at a time, each authority being responsible for a limited area of action. The hospital, for instance, has been cited as an organization with two lines of authority, one professional and one administrative,[16] and therefore it is suggested that it be regarded as a "functional" organization.

It seems that in professional organizations there are indeed two types of authority, but only the non-professional one is structured in a bureaucratic way, with a clear line and a center of authority. Various department heads (office, custodians, campus police, hospital kitchen, and the like) are subordinated to the administrative director and through him (in smaller organizations directly) to the head of the organization. This line is responsible mainly for secondary activities. Thus in professional organizations the staff or personnel performing secondary activities are administrators, clerks, and laborers, and this is the only part of the organization which has a clear line structure. The professionals who conduct the major goal activity do not form an authority structure in the regular sense of the term. As far as university research is concerned, each faculty member is to a very large extent free from any direct control by superiors. This holds to a large degree for the substance of his teaching as well. The physician's authority over the treatment given to his patient is a well-known fact.

Of course, there are many sources of control other than line orders and direct supervision of performance, especially a variety of rewards and sanctions exerted by informal pressures of peers. But most of these mechanisms also function in non-professional organizations, in addition to supervision, so that one can safely state that there is less control in professional organizations than in other organizations. Moreover, as far as the major goal activity is concerned, such control does not take the form of a hierarchy with superiors who issue orders and require performance reports. The typical professional is not under such control. This does not hold to the same extent for students, research assistants, and interns who are not part of the collegiate, peer-like, organizational structure.

There are three areas of activity in professional organizations: (a) major goal activities carried out by professionals and almost completely under the authority of the professional who performs the activity or directs the semi-professionals and non-professionals who perform it, (b) secondary activities performed by administrators and non-professional personnel under their control, and (c) secondary activities performed by the professionals.

[15] Wilbert E. Moore, *Industrial Relations and the Social Order*, rev. ed. (New York: Macmillan, 1951), pp. 77–84.

[16] H. L. Smith, "Two Lines of Authority Are One Too Many," *Modern Hospital* (1955), 84:54–64. See also J. Henry, "The Formal Structure of A Psychiatric Hospital," *Psychiatry* (1954), 17: 139–151.

administrative and professional authority

The latter include preparing statistics, participating in public-relations activities, and allocating facilities. In the first area there is no established hierarchy; in the second area the hierarchy does not involve professionals. In the third area there is often a clear hierarchy and administrative predominance, and here it is easy to misunderstand the nature of the professional organization and to see the professionals as part of an administrative line structure. But so far as a hierarchy exists in this realm, it is limited to secondary activities; so far as the main goal activities are concerned, there is much autonomy for professional authority.

In sum the dilemma of combining professional and administrative authority is handled in professional organizations by dividing the responsibilities so that the goal activities are controlled by the professionals, the means activities by the administrators, with the whole structure supervised by a middleman who has greater administrative skills and authority than the average professional, but more professional authority and competence than the average administrator because of his professionally oriented administrative training and experience. Still, there is no complete solution to this dilemma; studies of professional organizations report strains on this score, especially in those areas where professional considerations clash with means considerations.

The Semi-professional Organizations

The basis of professional authority is knowledge, and the relationship between administrative and professional authority is largely affected by the amount and kind of knowledge the professional has. The relationship described above holds largely for organizations in which professional authority is based on long training (5 years or more), when questions of life and death and/or privileged communication are involved, and when knowledge is created or applied rather than communicated. When professional authority is based on shorter training, involves values other than life or privacy, and covers the communication of knowledge, we find that it is related to administrative authority in a different way. First, professional work here has less autonomy; that is, it is more controlled by those higher in ranks and less subject to the discretion of the professional than in full-fledged professional organizations, though it is still characterized by greater autonomy than blue- or white-collar work. Second, the semi-professionals often have skills and personality traits more compatible with administration, especially since the qualities required for communication of knowledge are more like those needed for administration than those required for the creation and, to a degree, application of knowledge. Hence these organizations are run much more frequently by the semi-professionals themselves than by others.

The most typical semi-professional organization is the primary school. The social-work agency is the other major semi-professional organization. A semi-professional sector, rather than full-fledged organization, is found in the nursing service of hospitals.

The goal of the primary school is largely to communicate rather than to create or apply knowledge. The training of its professionals on the average falls well below 5 years of professional education. The social-work agency is less typical since it applies knowledge but is semi-professional in the fairly short training involved, in the fact that no questions of life and death are involved, and that privilege communication is not strictly maintained (e.g., *vis-à-vis* the courts). Among social workers, the longer the training and the more professional the orientation, the greater the tendency to orient to the social-work "profession" and not to the agency (the organization).

Graduate Work and Location
of Reference Groups (in Percentage)

Graduate Training in Social Work	Reference Group	
	Outside Agency (N = 25)	Inside Agency (N = 61)
Yes	56	36
No	44	64
N = 100%		

Peter M. Blau and W. Richard Scott, *Formal Organizations* (San Francisco: Chandler, 1962), p. 67.

Nurses apply knowledge, but their training is much shorter than doctors, and the question of what therapy to administer is concentrated in the hands of the doctors; in this sense the nursing service is not directly related to professional decisions of life or death, although nurses have much more effect on it than teacher or social worker, and in this sense are less-typical semi-professionals.

The work of these three groups has less autonomy than that of the professions discussed earlier. Their work day is tightly regulated by the organization; their duties at work are comparatively highly specified. In cases where performance is not visible—e.g., in the case of social work because it is. done in the field, or teaching because it is conducted in the classroom—detailed reporting on performance is required, and supervisors are allowed to make surprise visits to check on work being done. Nurses are directly observed and corrected by doctors and by superior nurses. Such supervision is not characteristic of the mechanisms of control found in the full-fledged professions. Inspectors are not widely used to drop in on a professor's classroom to check his teaching, especially not in the better universities. No doctor will be asked to report to an administrative superior on why he carried out his medical duties in the way he did or stand corrected by him. External examinations used in schools to check on teachers as well as students are very rare in universities.

Furthermore, much of the supervision is done by people who are themselves semi-professionals or professionals. Almost all school principals have been teachers; few have been recruited directly from training courses for school

administrative and professional authority

administration, and almost none are lay administrators. Virtually all social-work supervisors have been social workers. Few have assumed supervisory positions early in their careers and again almost none are lay administrators. The same is true of nursing. Thus while the semi-professionals are more supervised than the professionals, supervision is more often conducted by their own kind.

Some de-professionalization occurs in these organizations, as it does in full professional ones. Those teachers who are less committed to children, that is, the least "client-oriented," are more administration-conscious, and more likely to become principals. Few principals, unless the school is particularly small, keep teaching other than in a very limited, ritualistic way. Similarly, the social-work supervisors tend to be more organization-oriented, less client-oriented even in their field-work days, and they see few cases, if any, once they move up in the hierarchy.

Not all the differences between professional and semi-professional organizations can be traced to the differences in the nature of the professional authority. Part of the problem is due to the fact that the typical professional is a male whereas the typical semi-professional is a female. Despite the effects of emancipation, women on the average are more amenable to administrative control than men. It seems that on the average, women are also less conscious of organizational status and more submissive in this context than men. They also, on the average, have fewer years of higher education than men, and their acceptance into the medical profession or university teaching is sharply limited. It is difficult to determine if the semi-professional organizations have taken the form they have because of the high percentage of female employees, or if they recruit females because of organizational reasons; in all likelihood these factors support each other.

Whatever the deeper reasons, the fact is that the professional and administrative authority are here related in a different way from professional organizations. Control through organization regulations and superiors is much more extensive, though not as extensive as that of blue- or white-collar workers, and it is done mainly by semi-professionals themselves. As in professional organizations, the articulation of the two modes of authority is not without strain. Here, the semi-professional subordinates tend to adopt the full-fledged professions as their reference group in the sense that they view themselves as full-fledged professionals and feel that they should be given more discretion and be less controlled. Teachers resent the "interference" of principals and many principals try to minimize it. Social workers rebel against their supervisors. Nurses often feel that they are more experienced than the young intern or more knowledgeable than the older supervisor, and hence should not be expected to submit themselves to the command of either.

Service Organizations for Professionals

A less common way of combining advantages of organizational rationality with the use of professional knowledge is found in one type of research organization and in one type of hospital. The service research organization is usually attached to, or is part of, a university; it has no professional staff of its own. Professionals, usually members of the faculty of the university, are provided in this structure with computers, laboratories, clerical and research assistance, and other means which their work requires; but they are neither employed by the service organization nor are under its control. On the contrary, as a rule a faculty committee constitutes the organization's board of directors and directs its lay or professionally oriented administrator and semi-professional staff in arranging the facilities so as to increase the effectiveness of the services rendered.

Service research organizations should be distinguished from professional research organizations in which professionals constitute the major full-time personnel. These professionals are usually under some administrative control in terms of the projects carried out, the pace of work, and the audience toward which its output is oriented (e.g., paying clients *vs.* the professional community). It is in this kind of organization that one finds most often a faculty leader who combines his personal and professional influence with his control of the administrative structure. This organization is much more an organization *of* professionals than one *for* professionals. Between the two poles of service and professional research organizations there are various "middle" types, combining some of the characteristics of both types.

The main source of strain in the service research organization is that the organization, as the source of means, has very little control over the output, and hence is largely at the mercy of the professionals. On the other hand, the professional research organization finds it difficult to hold on to its full-fledged professionals because of the comparatively extensive control it exercises. Given the same economic and work conditions, few faculty members would willingly become members of such research organizations, but many staff members of professional research organizations would choose to join university faculties. In part this is due to the fact that there is greater prestige attached to university affiliation and to the title of professor, than that enjoyed by the staff of research organizations. But in part it is a consequence of trying to combine professional work by highly trained and creative professionals with more than usual administrative control.

Proprietary hospitals and clinics owned by groups of doctors are similar to service research organizations in that they provide the physicians with facilities, such as nursing staff, clerks, rooms, laboratory services, and instruments. Here doctors are members of the board of directors, and the proprietors. They control the administration of the hospital. The strain here is often the reverse of what it is in the professional organizations we formerly discussed. The doctors feel that they are wasting their time on administrative work, and conflict is prolonged by the lack of a neutral agent to arbitrate differences of opinion and interests among the professionals. Finally, there is no separation of the profit motive and professional interests since the doctors own these organizations. This often has displacement effects on the professional goals of these organizations. Low-quality care is more frequent in proprietary hospitals than in public or voluntary hospitals. Thus, even when professionals own and direct their own professional organizations, the conflict between administrative and professional authority cannot be eliminated; it exists within each doctor and among them.

90

administrative and professional authority

Contextual Factors

Every comparative statement made throughout this discussion should be read as though prefaced by the clause "all other conditions being equal." But since they never are equal, some of these conditions and the effects of their variation should be spelled out.

Externalization vs. Internalization

All organizations rely to some degree on other organizations and collectivities for the fulfillment and regulation of some of their functions. The point of interest here is which functions are handled by the professional organization and which are externalized. The more that professional functions are internalized and administrative functions externalized, the closer the organization comes to the ideal type of professional or semi-professional organization. The school is particularly close to the ideal type. It has few administrative problems to begin with because its scope is narrow. It relies considerably on families, community, social workers, police, and others to minister to most of the non-professional needs of its clients. Hospitals, on the other hand, have a broad scope: They take care of most of the non-professional needs of their patients. Hence hospitals have a greater percentage of non-professional staff and many more administrative problems than schools. Universities are from this viewpoint similar to schools. Boarding schools, on the other hand, are very different in their personnel structure and administrative problems because they are so broad in scope.

Research organizations differ considerably among themselves in terms of the externalization vs. the internalization of non-professional functions. Some research organizations are incorporated into university structures to a high degree, as for instance the Institute of Industrial Relations at the University of California, and many of their administrative functions are externalized. Other research organizations are comparatively independent and have to finance their activities themselves, as for instance the Stanford Research Institute. This type usually has a stronger administrative control structure.

At the other end of the continuum are research organizations that are incorporated into non-professional and even authoritarian organizations, such as the armed forces. As several studies show, there seems to be considerable confusion in the structure of these research organizations. Military principles of organization and behavior are mixed with professional ones. Strict observation of the protocol of the military hierarchy is demanded in some situations and professional, collegial relations are encouraged in others. The heads of many research organizations in the United States armed forces are professionally oriented administrators. This can be explained in part by the fact that although these research units are broad in scope, they rely to a large degree on other military units for supply and for regulation of many of their non-professional needs. Thus, administrative problems are minimized.

Of special interest from this viewpoint is a study which examines the

administrative and professional authority

effect of nationalization on the organizational structure of hospitals in England. The study shows that, when administrative responsibilities were taken over by a higher-level administrative unit, the heads of subordinated hospitals became more professionally oriented.[17] This can be compared to the relationships between the superintendent's office and the school principal. As more administrative tasks are taken over by the superintendent, the principal can devote more time and energy to his professional function: improving the quality of teaching.

Single vs. Multiple Professions

Another factor which impinges on the balance between professionals and administrators, and on the relationship between this balance and the process of goal implementation, is the number of professions cooperating in one organization and their mutual attitudes. The greater the number and the higher the tensions among the various professions, the greater is the need for a neutral administrator as final authority. The grammar school is from this point of view on one end of the continuum, with one professional group, the teachers. The university is on the other end, with a large number of professional groups (departments). When there is strong rivalry among various groups of faculty, as for instance between humanities and natural sciences, a layman is often more functional as a university president than is a professional. In general, the university administrator functions often as an arbitrator among different professional groups.

Hospitals are in the middle of the continuum. General hospitals are closer to the school from this viewpoint because they are dominated by one profession. Mental hospitals are closer to the universities because of their multiprofessional nature, with an uneasy dominance by psychiatrists. The overlapping functions of psychiatrists, clinical psychologists, psychiatric social workers, and physical therapists, as well as the different schools of treatment, make a neutral administrator highly functional in many mental hospitals.

Private vs. Public Organizations

One of the most important dimensions for the study of professional organizations is the way they are owned and financed. Many professional organizations are partly financed through contributions or from tax money. Clients' fees play very different roles in various organizations; in some cases they have no role at all and in others they are the most influential criterion for action. Another aspect of the same problem is the way the professionals are compensated. In some cases they are paid salaries, in others fees, by the organization or by the clients. These factors impinge on the relationships between the administrators and the professionals, especially in organizations with a profit goal, because they determine to a considerable degree who represents the goal—the professionals or the administrators.

From the viewpoint of professional goals, the distorting potential of a lay administrator seems to be highest in those "private" professional organi-

[17] C. Sofer, "Reactions to Administrative Change," *Human Relations* (1955), 8: 229.

administrative and professional authority

zations where professionals are salaried. On the other hand, in those public organizations where the professionals are not salaried and the administrators represent public interests, the distorting potential may be minimized. Between these two poles exists a whole gamut of alternatives. Almost no studies exist of the effects of these various arrangements on the relation between professional and administrative authority.

administrative and professional authority

modern
organization
and the client
nine

The ideal of service to the public prevails in our society; it is derived in the main from the ideal of the maximum happiness of the greatest number.[1] By definition, public services are assumed to have been established in order to supply services to the public. The private economy is seen as geared to the needs and wishes of the consumer. This ideology reflects a traditional classical theory of economics which holds that only an enterprise which serves the consumer can survive and that the consumer controls the production and the distribution of goods and services through his purchasing power. But it leaves unanswered the empirical question of the degree to which public and private organizations are actually tuned to citizen and consumer needs, and of the ways in which these needs are effectively expressed.

Separation of Consumption from Control

Modern society is characterized by a highly advanced division of labor and by bureaucratization. Fused elements become separated and function independently. Each differentiation raises the question: What are the relations among the separated elements? One of the best-known studies of such a process is that of Berle and Means on the separation of

[1] This Chapter is based on an article by the author first published in the *Administrative Science Quarterly*, 1958.

94

control from ownership.[2] Berle and Means demonstrate that when an economic enterprise becomes incorporated and bureaucratized, the control over the enterprise (or organization) becomes separated from the right to its profits. Both elements had been integrated in the concepts of private property and entrepreneurship. Their separation raises the problem of the relationship between the two elements, the one invested in the roles of managers and the other in the roles of stockholders.

Specialization and bureaucratization, the multiplication of organizations, have caused another split. The customer's role, considered as one element in the ideology discussed above and in the classical model of economics, has been divided into two: *consumption*, in the sense of receiving services and goods for the satisfaction of one's needs, and *control* over the distribution of resources in accordance with one's needs. While consumption has been retained by the consumer (like dividends by the stockholder), control has been, to some degree, taken from the consumer and invested in other roles (like control over production in Berle and Means' analysis).

The various economic organizations may be arranged on a continuum according to the degree of separation between consumption and control. The smallest degree of control by consumers will be found in public monopolies (e.g., the post office); next are public services such as public schools, universities, hospitals, health services, and social-welfare agencies; then come private monopolies, duopolies, and oligopolies; relatively high consumer control will be found in the economy of small business.

One important way in which the process of separation is revealed is the separation of consumption from direct financing, common to most public organizations. The agencies producing and supplying public services do not depend on consumers' fees in any manner similar to that conceived by the classical model of economics and by the service ideology. In many cases the fee charged is a small proportion of the actual price of the service, as, for example, tuition fees in many universities or charges of public hospitals. Services are financed through taxation or private endowments.

Sometimes taxation is considered an indirect form of consumers' fee. But this indirect way of financing (as compared to direct financing through purchasing) implies that *control is at least partially invested in those who recruit the financial means from the public and allocate them to the producers of the service.* This is even more true in the case of private endowments in which reports to the contributors concerning the utilization of funds are generally less frequent and extensive than they are in the case of taxation.

The term "public" suggests the image of one and the same public consuming services for which it has paid through taxation and endowments, whereas it is well known that there is not one public but many publics, and the financing public often only partially overlaps the public that consumes that particular service, and vice versa. Although there is considerable variation, the degree to which a given segment of the public consumes public services is inversely related to its participation in financing. Higher strata pay more taxes than lower strata, but benefit less from public services.

[2] A. A. Berle and G. C. Means, *The Modern Corporation and Private Property* (New York: Macmillan, 1933).

It is also significant that tax payments are involuntary and cannot be withheld when services are unsatisfactory, and that endowments are generally induced by motives other than the satisfaction expected from the respective services. Thus, in public organizations, one source of control, that deriving from financing, is at least partially separated from consumption of these services.

Separating financing from consumption is only one way of separating control from consumption. Another way is public and private monopolization. The post office, for instance, charges fees which tend to cover all the expenses of the service supplied, but that does not mean that the post office administration is dependent on the consumer more than the university is dependent on the student or the state hospital on the patient. There is no satisfactory substitute (in the same category of price and convenience) for the services of the post office. Consequently the consumer has little direct control over the service. This seems to hold for public organizations in general; that is, for the service provided by 11,000,000 public servants, in local, state, and federal organizations.

The separation of consumption from control is not a problem of public administration or of public services and monopolies only, but one of bureaucratization in general. It applies to the private economy as well, although in varying degrees. The problem of exploitation of consumers by private monopolies is only too well known. A similar relative indifference to the needs of consumers arises in duopolies and oligopolies, such as the big TV networks, especially when price leadership, price fixing, and similar processes operate. To these we should add corporations which produce mainly for one big consumer (often the armed forces). These corporations are relatively indifferent to the mass of small individual consumers.[3] But even small competitive firms do not allocate their resources solely according to the dollar votes of consumers. In addition to consumers, they have to satisfy government regulations, taxation, trade unions, stockholders, and financiers, to mention only the more important groups. They tend to allocate their resources according to the relative pressures exerted by these various forces.

The consumer is therefore only one source of pressure among many, and certainly not the most organized and powerful one. The assumption that what maximizes the consumer's satisfaction is also best for all the others concerned, as the classical model of economics implies and as some people still believe, is as often wrong as it is right. For instance, higher wages for workers are likely to bring higher prices for consumers. More profit for the producer may mean poorer or more costly products for the consumer. The distinction among consumers, producers and savers, is an analytical one and resembles the distinction sociologists make among different roles played by the same person. But the fact that many persons are both producers and consumers does not mean that there can be no economic act which is advantageous for the one and unfavorable to the other. First, some people, such as children and the

---

[3] The same point has been made for other categories of corporations. "Large firms producing finished consumers' goods are not ordinarily subject to serious *direct* pressure from this group—either from middlemen or ultimate consumers." R. A. Gordon, *Business Leadership in the Large Corporation* (Berkeley: University of California Press, 1961), p. 253.

modern organization and the client

aged, are consumers only. Second, most economic acts are advantageous for the producers of some goods or services and disadvantageous for the consumers of these or some other products, and these two groups of people are, in most cases, not identical.

The consumer's direct control is greatest in retail stores, small business, and small service agencies (such as barber shops), where commissions and tips play a role. These are also the economic units in which separation of ownership and management is the least pronounced—i.e., the economic organizations in which the processes of bureaucratization and differentiation are least developed.

The professionals are difficult to place in this continuum. Their services, especially when organized in any administrative form, are separate from the fee charged and therefore from direct pressure by the client. Here separation between consumption and control is supported by a strong ideology, sometimes taken over by other branches of organizational society; namely, that those who administer the service are in a better position to judge what is good for the consumer than he is himself; hence separation of control from consumption is the best way to maximize the happiness of the greatest number. We now turn to an examination of this argument.

The Consequences
of Consumption-Control Separation

The separation of consumption from control has many consequences that few would consent to do without. In many areas consumers are indeed incapable of judging what is best for them. Separating consumption from control opens the possibility for control to be exercised by an authority that is better able to satisfy the consumer's needs. The consumer's plight has various sources. Sometimes it is due to his relative ignorance, as in the case of patient and physician; in other instances it is a question of the need for means of enforcing organizational norms, as in the case of the university which determines entrance standards; in still other cases it is a question of long-run versus short-run interests of the consumer; like the stockholder, the consumer is often on the side of the short-run interests, while those in control of production are often aware of the need not to subordinate all the available resources to higher dividends or better and cheaper products, but to allocate a certain proportion to reinvestment and innovation. The consumer cannot be relied upon to look after these organizational needs, although in the long run he may benefit from their being satisfied.

The separation of consumption from control is also a necessary condition for much of what is called social justice. Through progressive taxation and administrative decrees it becomes possible for the public to influence the allocation of the national income. In short, the separation of control from consumption has many consequences widely considered desirable.

This brings up the question: Should this process be encouraged or minimized? This is a question of the relative realization of values which are only partially consistent. If in view of his superior knowledge the administrator or the expert takes control, the consumer's freedom of choice is re-

97

stricted in the name of other values such as health, education, or increased possibilities of choice in the future. The question of the extent to which this freedom of choice should be sacrificed for other values is a value judgment that cannot be made here. But it seems relevant to point out that freedom of choice is often sacrificed without any real gain in terms of other values. Once control is withdrawn from the consumer, there arises a tendency on the part of the organization to expand the area of its control for illegitimate reasons, such as the power drive of some bureaucrats, and the ease of handling controlled clients as compared to clients with more freedom of choice.

Thus, for example, one may support or oppose hospital uniforms for patients when the issue of disinfecting is involved, but there can be little justification for limiting the choice of clothes in homes for the aged. In school children have to be controlled for their own good. But when such attitudes and techniques are extended to PTA meetings, they become illegitimate.

We can now ask: What mechanisms limit the separation of consumption and control and confine control within its functional and legitimate boundaries?

The Problem
of Relating Consumption to Control

The process of bureaucratization differentiates elements which formerly were fused. This raises the problem of re-establishing a relationship among these elements. This is not likely to be done by reinvesting full control in the consumer (by re-merging the elements), as this would undermine the values discussed above. Rather the function has to be fulfilled by institutionalized bridges: the elements remain separated but not unrelated. The consumers do not exercise full control themselves, but they exert influence on those in control.

Communication Bridges

One interesting problem is the degree of effectiveness of communication lines between the clients and producers, especially in public organizations, large corporations, and other highly bureaucratized enterprises.[4] We suggest that in many cases few lines of institutionalized communication exist. How much communication flows from the clients of the post office to the postmaster? How many communicative contacts between patients and top hospital administrators are more than accidental or formalistic?

A second question is: When communication does exist, how representative is it of the clients' actual feelings and needs? We suggest that often it is highly unrepresentative. Extreme cases are morning radio programs intended for housewives, which broadcast songs selected according to statistics

[4] For an interesting study of this kind, see Morris Janowitz and William Delany, "The Bureaucrat and the Public: A Study of Informational Perspectives," *Administrative Science Quarterly* (1957), 2:141–162.

modern organization and the client

of popularity based on the number of coins inserted into juke boxes by teen-agers. Relatively more meaningful are the indexes which make and break television programs, yet in most cases are known to be unreliable and un-representative. Many of the market-research programs are unsatisfactory from a professional viewpoint. The "letter to the editor," "suggestion box," and other channels of complaints are also highly unrepresentative. In very few organizations[5] does informal communication concerning consumers' needs reach the higher levels of the organization and get transmitted to those who could act on it. One of the important reasons for this seems to be an institu-tionalized insensitivity to the consumer, discussed below.

The relation between consumer and supplier of goods and services may be further analyzed with regard to the communicative influence and skill of the various types of consumers. Some consumers are more communicative than others (e.g., journalists) and, therefore, frequently receive better services. Exploration of the mechanisms involved here may demonstrate the signifi-cance of nets of communication for the problem at hand. Journalists, like others in the communications field, cut short the communication system by communicating the consumer's needs to top management directly. In this way top management is often informed of issues which would not have reached it through the regular channels of communication. There seem to be other, more institutionalized, short cuts as well; for instance, surprise control-checks, interviews of customers by high-ranking managers, and "shoppers" planted by management. When these mechanisms are studied, their relative merits have to be compared not only from the point of view of their communicative virtues but also with regard to their effectiveness in exerting pressure, since communications alone might prove ineffective. From this standpoint there appears to be little substitution for an aggressive press, although the latter's potential threat often suffices to make other channels of communication effective. To what extent the press and other mass media are free to criticize major services and producers who have large advertising accounts or strong political connections has so far been a matter of much comment but little systematic study.

Institutionalized Attitudes to Consumers

The service ideology implies that those who serve the consumer accept this ideology, are rewarded for behavior conforming to its standards, and are deprived for deviating from it. Actually, some basic features of organizations make service norms difficult to reinforce. Some characteristics of organizations even make for *insensitivity* to the consumer.

Many lower-level clerks and sales workers who come into contact with customers are organization-oriented and not customer-oriented. A study of retail grocery workers reports that when asked about the "most important single factor in present job," 22 per cent mentioned "like associates," 22 per cent supervision, 29 per cent future advancement, and only 5 per cent contact with customers.[5] Thus it appears that co-workers and supervisors with whom clerks and sales workers interact intimately (as compared to the relatively

[5] Mason Haire and Josephine P. Gottsdanker, "Factors Influencing Industrial Morale," *Personnel* (1951), 27:445–454, esp. p. 447.

impersonal contact with customers) are often the "significant others" toward whom they are sensitized. Similarly, social workers more oriented to their team seem to treat their relief clients in a more impersonal manner, as shown in the following table.

Cohesion of a Group of Social Workers
Relating Popularity in This Group
to Client-Orientation (in Percentage)

Client-Orientation	Group Cohesion			
	High		Low	
	Individual's Popularity		Individual's Popularity	
	High (N = 17)	Low (N = 12)	High (N = 14)	Low (N = 17)
Impersonal N = 100%	62	66	30	20

Peter M. Blau and W. Richard Scott, *Formal Organizations* (San Francisco: Chandler, 1962), p. 108.

This would be of little consequence if promotion, supervisors' approval, and co-workers' attitudes were geared to service orientation toward customers or clients. But it seems that promotion and other supervisory sanctions depend partly on other factors (e.g., obedience), while co-workers' attitudes are more influenced by other values such as friendliness and loyalty.[6]

Sensitivity to the client may often be disadvantageous for the organization man. If, when confronted with an irregular case, he rigidly sticks to the organization's norms, he usually fares better than if he tries to bend the norms of the organization to the client's needs or if he bothers his superiors with the case. Furthermore, contact with clients is usually relatively concentrated on the lower levels of the organization; those who are successful in their relations with clients may find it more difficult to attain promotion than those who prepare themselves for the next, less-client-oriented stage by being more organization- than client-minded. To sum up: To be overly client-oriented and to transmit clients' demands upward is a relatively unrewarding experience in many organizations.

Sensitivity to the client seems to be greater in cases in which the relationship is more intimate, where the client is significant as an agent of rewards and deprivations. The relationship between clerk and client in the post office is very impersonal. But the relationship between a tailor and a permanent customer is intimate. Restaurants, for instance, may be fruitfully classified according to the clientele to which they cater; they range all the way from

6 "Unfortunately, management has paid little attention to consumption studies up to now." Irwin Friend and Irving B. Kraves, "New Light on the Consumer Market," *Harvard Business Review* (1957), 35:105.

100

modern organization and the client

railway-station restaurants, which often are quite indifferent to their transitory customers, to exclusive restaurants, which conscientiously cater to a selected group of regular clients.

From the viewpoint of intimate *vs.* impersonal elements, the relationship may be asymmetrical as between professionals and their clients. This means that tension is built into the structure of the situation, since the client expects the relation to be more personal than the professional is able or willing to make it. Another variation on the same line of the personal-impersonal continuum is the pseudo-personal relationship created by salesmen. This is an attempt on the part of the supplier of goods to manipulate the consumer by simulating an intimate relationship—i.e., creating the impression that the relationship is symmetric, based on mutual responsibility (and hence mutual control) while actually the relationship is asymmetrical (controlled by one side).

Co-optation and Communication

Organizations which are committed to the ideology of service and are aware of the problems of communication with consumers, especially when they wish to communicate a message to the consumers because they need their cooperation, sometimes apply a method known as co-optation.[7] Customers' representatives are invited to participate in the decision-making process. In certain cities in Belgium, for example, the customers elect a representative to participate in a transportation council that regulates public transportation.[8]

The conditions under which co-optation is real and the conditions under which it is fictitious are not firmly established. It seems that co-optation is more often applied in communications from those in control to the clients than the other way around. Co-optation is often used in order to create a semblance of communication from clients to those in control, without actually providing for effective communication. Thus, although co-optation is theoretically a mechanism of consumers' influence, it is frequently not applied so as to realize its potentials. When co-optation is manipulated or fictitious, it not only fails to co-optate the consumer, but blocks the expression of his needs. Simulated co-optation suggests that the communication problem has been solved, whereas actually it only conceals the need for real communication and influence.

Molding the Consumer's Desires

The problem of the gap in communication between the consumer and those who control his consumption is sometimes partially "solved" when the organization, which provides its product or service, also molds the consumer's desires. Although basic needs are difficult to mold, the manner in which they are satisfied seems to be quite open to manipulation. Furthermore, additional needs are created simultaneously with the means of

[7] Philip Selznick, *T.V.A. and the Grass Roots* (Berkeley: University of California Press, 1949).

[8] On consumer councils see C. A. R. Crosland, *The Future of Socialism* (London: Cape, 1956), p. 470.

satisfying them. Thus, to the extent that the supplier of goods and services is able to create satisfaction, there is little need for communication from the consumer to the controller. This, of course, is a complete reversal of the process as depicted by the service ideology, according to which the consumer's choice determines the allocation of resources. The governmental agencies are also engaged in producing a satisfied "clientele." By 1948, according to an estimate by the Bureau of the Budget, 45,000 persons were engaged by the federal government (directly or indirectly) in dispersing publicity and information, at an annual salary of $13,043,452.[9] But so far the methods of persuasion have been only partially successful; therefore our basic problem of bridging the elements separated by bureaucratization still exists.

The Countervailing Power of the Consumer

The mechanisms discussed up to this point are mainly mechanisms of communication which transmit or fail to transmit the required information concerning consumers' wishes. But communication is likely to be ineffective unless reinforced by power. Therefore it is necessary to analyze the sources and channels of the consumers' power to countervail other pressures on those in control. There are two main types of such power—economic and political.

1. The economic countervailing power of the consumer is different in different parts of the economy. Following the continuum presented above, we might say that it is large for retail shops and small-scale private services, smaller for large, bureaucratized enterprises, especially those depending only partially on the mass of individual consumers, and even smaller for the rest of the economy, including organized professionals and private and public monopolies.

Countervailing power discussed so far is that of the unorganized, random activity of the mass of small individual consumers. Sometimes the term is applied to the organized activity of consumers. Although such activity occurs in some extreme cases of exploitation, it is very rare. Most consumers have only a fragmentary, limited interest in most products. They are unwilling to devote energy, time, and money to the aim of an organized consumers' strike. In most cases, such a strike is successfully organized, only if the service or product is invested with a broad and symbolic meaning, as in the boycott of the bus services in Montgomery, Alabama.

The assumption that certain economic organizations—e.g., department stores—act as natural consumers' agents, since they attempt to countervail the economic power of producers, seems open to serious question.[10] Generally the gains which these organizations achieve by exerting pressure on producers are gains for the organizations themselves. The consumer may or may not benefit from the power struggle between producer and distributor, but the latter cannot be considered his representative. Besides, a coalition of producers and distributors may be as likely as a conflict. Subordinating one

---

[9] John M. Pfiffner and Robert B. Presthus, *Public Administration* (New York: Ronald, 1960), p. 166.

[10] Compare J. K. Galbraith, *American Capitalism* rev. ed. (Boston: Houghton Mifflin, 1956).

102

modern organization and the client

party to the other (as in the gasoline and automobile industries) is also not uncommon. In these cases an understanding between these powerful partners often seems to occur at the expense of the consumer. Thus the consumer seems to be the one taken advantage of rather than the one served by the economy. If he possesses any significant, organized, countervailing power, it is, in most sectors of modern society, not economic but political.

2. The countervailing political power of the consumer is his ability to exert pressure on political authorities to intervene in economic processes in ways that will be advantageous to him. Although he has limited influence on those who serve him or on those who are in direct control over those who serve him, he has, under certain conditions, some indirect influence on those who direct or who manage and control the supply of goods and services. Many price regulations, safety standards, health standards, and advertising laws are created by politicians to satisfy voting consumers.[11] These controls are relatively indirect and regulative in private industry, but usually much stronger (although not necessarily strong enough) in cases where an industry is more monopolized (i.e., less under client control). In public organizations these controls are more direct and prescriptive.

Political mechanisms may be relatively effective, but their influence in democratic societies is limited since interference with economic processes is in general limited. But even in sectors which are under public control, this bridge is only partial because the mechanisms of communication between voters and politicians have all the deficiencies shown to be characteristic of the mechanisms of communication between consumers and those in direct control over the supply of goods and services. Take as an example the independent regulatory commissions which are supposed to represent the consuming public *vis à vis* various monopolies and other large-scale economic organizations. It is highly revealing to compare the National Labor Relations Board, which acts as a mediator between the organized camps of labor and management, to the other commissions, which stand between large corporations on one hand and an unorganized public on the other. A 1957–1958 hearing by a special House Sub-committee on Legislative Oversight reported: "1. Certain F.C.C. Commissioners had received full expenses for themselves and their wives to attend industry conventions and had also had various other expenses paid for by regulated industries. . . . 2. Commissioners had engaged in constant fraternization with individuals and corporations who appear as litigants before the Commission. . . ."[12] In the case of the N.L.R.B., such influence by management can be countered by labor unions, but who will counter the organized influence of industry in the case of the F.C.C. and the other commissions?

In order to reach a better understanding of these mechanisms, it is necessary to specify, for each major product or service, the consuming public, the voting public, the financing source, the producers, and the distributors of the respective products and services, and to study the relations among

[11] See J. M. Clark, "America's Changing Capitalism: The Interplay of Politics and Economics," in M. Berger, T. Abel and C. H. Page (eds.), *Freedom and Control in Modern Society* (Toronto: Van Nostrand, 1954), pp. 192–205.
[12] *The New York Times*, Jan. 28, 1958.

them. Of special interest here is the relation between consumers and voters. The assumption that these two groups are identical is oversimplified. Some consumers do not vote because they are too young. Others constitute an insignificant voting group because they fail to vote or their right to vote is denied, because the group of consumers of the specific product is small as compared to the general voting public, or because groups which exert counter-pressure are much stronger. Much of what has been said above concerning the various groups of consumers regarding their communication abilities also holds for the study of their countervailing political power. There is no one undifferentiated public. Some groups of consumers have much more political power than others. Students, for instance, are far more politically articulate than most clients of the social-welfare agencies. Finally, political loyalty, and voting in particular, in most cases depend on issues other than direct issues of consumption.

To sum up: To understand better the consumer's relation to control, the traditional organizational chart ought to be expanded in two directions: (a) The differentiation of consumer publics and their various contacts, lines of communication, and ways of exerting pressure are to be incorporated at one end. (b) The various "political" organs which control public organizations and regulate some privately owned organizations have to be brought into the frame on the other end, and the relationship between the consumer and these political authorities has to be analyzed. A more complete analysis such as this will show how much "service" by the organizations to clients is an ideology, and how much is organizational reality. Moreover it will suggest the conditions under which the service ideology can be realized.

modern organization and the client

organization and the social environment

ten

Under what social conditions do modern organizations rise and develop? What is society's role in regulating the relations among organizations? How will the relations between society and organizations change in the coming decades? These are highly complex questions and there are as yet few hard facts to guide us in answering them; and what is known is subject to revision as new findings are made.

The Organizational Revolution

Industrialization presages major changes in all societal sectors. A rise in educational standards and achievements, the spread of political consciousness, secularization, the rapid growth of science, the decline of the family, and increase in social mobility: all are associated with industrialization. We refer to all these related changes as "modernization." A central element of modernization is the development of many large organizations. Nearly half of the corporate wealth in the United States is in the hands of 200 large corporations. After all, factories were not simply structures to house new machines but also places where work relations assumed new form. The rise in education presupposed the emergence of schools and led to the development of universities. In politics, the party—a mass organization —took over what had been the exclusive domain of cliques and cabals. The bureaucratic state emerged from the ruins of feudal society. In all these areas, some organizations existed before the Industrial Revolution. The

Italian city-states had developed some fairly large and complex commercial organizations. Some universities existed in medieval Europe. State bureaucracies operated in ancient Egypt, in Imperial China, and in Byzantium. But these organizations were few in number, encompassing only a small fraction of the members of the society, and were not "pure" because many of the principles of effective organization—as specified by Classical theory of administration or the Weberian structuralist approach—were not observed. Recruitment to the Chinese bureaucracy was not based on specialized knowledge or other bureaucratic merits as much as it was on a general philosophical knowledge, with stress on the ability to recite and write poetry. Organizational positions were not separated from social status; recruitment was limited largely to the gentry. The allocation of rewards for organizational performance was not monopolized by the organization. In late medieval France, for instance, judges were compensated by the litigants rather than by the court. It is only with modernization that there emerged such a great number of organizations, characterized by a relative "purity" of structure, encompassing a large part of the population, and penetrating into a wide spectrum of social spheres. This is reflected by the fact that since 1940, in the United States, despite considerable and continuous growth, the number of self-employed workers in the labor force has remained about the same. In 1960 the population of self-employed workers in the American labor force was 15 per cent, compared to 23 per cent in 1910. It is estimated that half the labor force, about 25,000,000, worked for "big organizations." [1] Earlier societies had some organizations, but modern society is a society of organizations.

What were the conditions which fostered this growth of organizations? The main sociological characteristic of modernization is differentiation.[2] Differentiation is best viewed against the background of a primitive or traditional society. Small, simple societies fulfill the same basic social functions as large, complex ones, including production of goods and services (even if it only involves picking ripe bananas); allocation of products (even if only within the family); social integration (e.g., tribal rituals to keep the families together); and normative integration, which reinforces the members' commitment to their culture and encourages its transmission from generation to generation (even if this is largely a matter of handing down folklore by the elders to the younger members). The process of modernization is one in which old functions are more efficiently served rather than one in which new functions emerge. This gain in efficiency is largely achieved by differentiation, whereby the various functions which were carried out in one social unit, the extended family, come to be served by a number of distinct social units.

Differentiation is essential for the organizational revolution for two related reasons. First, it allows the establishment of new social units devoted to specific functions, especially those of production and allocation, leaving social and normative integration in the hands of older, more traditional units, above all the family. Second, it makes possible the formation of

---

[1] Robert Presthus, *The Organizational Society* (New York: Knopf, 1962), p. 74.
[2] Talcott Parsons and Neil J. Smelser, *Economy and Society* (Glencoe, Ill.: The Free Press, 1956).

organization and the social environment

"artificial" social units, deliberately designed for the efficient service of these functions; such units have a set of norms and a structure (including an authority hierarchy) which have been tooled to fit the specific goal or goals of the organization. Production, once carried out by the father and his sons, is now carried out in the factory, which is free to put younger men in charge of older ones, or group the workers in the order it finds efficient. Education is carried out by organizations in which teacher-student relations are formed according to what is considered as advancing education; they are not submerged in the elder-junior structure of the community. Even religion is largely removed from the family and tribe and invested in a structure which recruits persons whose religious leadership is more effective than that of the average father or chieftain. Allocation is not left to primitive barter exchange, but has developed into a highly complex and organized system.

Moreover, we now have secondary differentiation in each sphere—i.e., the emergence of sub-specialties each with an organizational structure geared to its own needs. Thus the vocational high school is different from the academic high school, and a mass-production corporation differs from a small business. All this is involved in structural differentiation by which rationalization of the service to the various social functions formerly concentrated in a single unit is advanced.

Paralleling the changes in societal structure was a deep cultural change which, like the structural change, both preceded and accompanied the organizational revolution. This culture change has been most extensively analyzed by Max Weber.[3] Weber sought to discover from what conditions the modern, rational, capitalistic system of production developed. He rejected the Marxist interpretation which saw the origin of capitalism in changes in technological factors and property relations. Weber stressed the influence of the rise of a new set of norms, which he called the Protestant Ethic. He noted that in Germany, Protestant children were more likely than Catholic children to attend commerical schools. He observed also that modern capitalism flourished first in Protestant countries such as England and the Netherlands rather than in Catholic countries. To an important degree, Weber's case rests on the substantive similarities he saw between Protestant (especially Calvinist) and capitalistic attitudes. For example, the Protestant is exhorted to hard work and to practice asceticism in this world, for the greater glory of God. The doctrine of predestination, central to Calvinism, encourages the believer to seek signs of his election, prominent among which is worldly and financial success. Hard work, thrift, and the emphasis on asceticism—which led to the re-investing of one's surplus income rather than to its expenditure for luxury items or non-productive prestige symbols, are also central requirements for nascent capitalism. Thus the behavior approved and encouraged by Protestantism and that called for by capitalism are very similar.[4]

Weber's inquiry into the origins of capitalism, which he saw as a rational form of the organization of production, is one of the most widely dis-

---

[3] Max Weber (Talcott Parsons, trans.), *The Protestant Ethic and the Spirit of Capitalism* (New York: Scribner, 1958).

[4] Weber offered support for his thesis in his cross-cultural studies. For a full discussion of Weber's work, see R. Bendix, *Max Weber: An Intellectual Portrait* (Garden City, N. Y.: Doubleday, 1960).

cussed studies in modern sociology. Less frequently considered is Weber's approach to the emergence of two other forms of rationality—science and bureaucratic organization. Weber saw the religious change supporting these developments as well. All three—capitalism, modern science, and bureaucratic organization—came to the forefront at about the same time in the same countries, and to a large degree supported one another's evolution.

The cultural conditions which provide a supportive setting for the development of modern organizations, science, and economy are not, however, limited to the Protestant faith; they are related to two broad normative themes which are found in a number of belief systems. One theme is worldliness. Religions, philosophies, and ideologies differ in the degree to which they orient human thoughts and efforts toward this world rather than the next, whether it be the Christian ideal of heaven or the state of nirvana. Rational behavior is encouraged by worldliness and discouraged by other-worldliness, since it requires an empirical reference, a reality testing, found only in this world. Second, rationality is encouraged by asceticism. The building of a modern economy, the pursuit of scientific research, the operation of an efficient organization: all require a commitment to long-run rather than short-run goals. If the yields of a young economy are immediately absorbed by consumption without re-investment, there will be no economic growth. If a scientist seeking a quick solution to a difficult problem violates the canons of empirical research, his findings will not be valid. If a bureaucrat is regularly guided by his emotions or kinship considerations rather than by established rules and procedures, the organization will be inefficient. A tolerance for frustration, a certain amount of asceticism, is essential for the success of rational behavior and rational social units. Protestantism abetted the organizational revolution because it combined the two values of worldliness and asceticism. Other religious and secular belief systems, though different in substance from Protestantism, have expressed these values too. It is these two normative themes rather than a particular religion, which provide the cultural context for the organizational revolution and growth.

Cultural and social changes often find a parallel in psychological changes, although not in a one-to-one relationship. That is, modern man is different from one who lives in a primitive or traditional society. He has the psychological prerequisites of an effective "organization man." Persons who have grown up and lived in closed communities are adjusted to a social structure in which all relationships—both peer and authority—are closely articulated. Warner, in his study of a small community, observed that one group occupied the major positions in the stratification system (upper classes), in the municipal government, and in the town's industrial and business organizations, where they were both owners and managers, while another group constituted the lower classes, the voters who would never be elected to public office, and the workers.[5] This fusion of positions in different social spheres allowed the power elite to maintain total control in the community, while it gave to the worker a sense of security: His peer and authority relations were consistent in all social spheres as were the basic social norms which

[5] W. L. Warner and J. O. Low, *The Social System of the Modern Factory* (New Haven: Yale University Press, 1947).

organization and the social environment

guided his behavior; and although excluded from the community's real decision-making process, he had a sense that "things were being taken care of," with little expenditure of effort on his part. In short, totalistic control was often paternalistic and the lower classes were adjusted to it.

But modern organizational society requires a different kind of personality—one that is accustomed to shuttling back and forth between different social units, especially between the family and the residential community on the one hand and work organizations on the other, and between systems that differ in their peer and authority relations (e.g., one's peer in one system may be a superior in another), and among which many norms are not transferred. And not only is the modern personality adapted to such shifting in its daily and weekly life cycle, but it benefits from the shifting, for tensions built up in one realm can be released in another. A worker or executive releases tensions accumulated at work in his after-work social and familial relations, and he releases at work some of the tensions generated at home. (One cartoonist illustrated this point by showing, in one panel, a wife welcoming her husband with, "Dear, how was your day at the office?" and, in the second panel, his secretary welcoming him with, "Dear, how was your night at home?")

The second major feature of the modern personality, especially of the "organization man," is a high tolerance for frustration and the ability to defer gratification. It is this psychological quality which is basic to a large variety of more specific and concrete psychological features that are needed for rational organizational work. It supports the habit of appearing at work regularly and of working at a routine task at an even pace. It makes it possible for the worker to disregard personal preferences and ties, thus enchancing the treatment of clients as "cases." In instances of conflict among departments, divisions, or ranks, it makes possible solution by appeal to the law or to rules or by compromise, rather than by "fighting it out."

A third related psychological feature is the achievement orientation; i.e., the psychic urge to achieve higher material and symbolic rewards. The organization is characterized by a variety of status-sequences or "careers" in which rewards are ordered in an increasing fashion to reward the organization man for conforming to the rules and performing his tasks well. However, this device as a mechanism for inducing cooperation and conformity is effective only if the individual is anxious to gain the rewards. The achievement orientation is also crucial for the long process of education and training required for participation in many organizational roles, especially professional ones. Without the desire for the higher rewards involved in higher organizational (and social) status, an individual would hardly subject himself to the economic and status losses inflicted by the long educational preparation required for many organizational positions.

While the ability to defer gratification and the desire for achievement are important qualities of the organization man, organizational participants differ considerably with respect to each of these characteristics and the way in which they are combined, as well as on many other personality factors. In this sense, there is no one organizational personality but a range of types which find in different positions and in different organizations an opportunity to express their varying needs. Persons who shun company may find jobs as night watchmen, or as researchers in isolated laboratories; gregarious persons may become star salesmen. A person who is highly motivated to achieve may rise in an organization while another person, who is less achievement-oriented, may be content to remain in a position, say that of foreman. Still, by and large, for most organizational positions, especially those above the lower levels, a fair share of the basic qualities discussed above contribute, though in different degree, to the adjustment of the person to the organization and to the organization's effectiveness.

The fact that most people in organizations have the requisite psychological characteristics for organizational life is in part a result of selective recruitment by which the organization rejects or removes those whose personalities make them unfit to participate. The major credit for this convergence of personality and organizational requirements, however, must go to the modern family and the modern educational system, both of which produce the type of person who will make a good organization man. The middle-class stress on the values of punctuality, neatness, integrity, consistency, the accent on conformity, and above all achievement, are the foundation of the qualities which facilitate adjustment to organizational demands. The organization's effectiveness with respect to this aspect of the recruitment and placing of personnel is due more to the social environment which provides the "right" kind of participants than to any deliberate efforts by the organization to shape personalities according to its needs.

Organizational Interaction and Social Environment

Modern society is a society of organizations, but the obvious question of how these organizations interact has not been systematically explored. We know a great deal about interaction among persons, something about interaction among groups, but surprisingly little about interaction among organizations. Hence much of the following formulation is highly tentative.

Relations among organizations are to some extent regulated by the state which in its laws, administrative agencies, courts, and regulatory commissions sets the limits within which organizations act and interact. Societies differ greatly in the degree to which they control their economies; the same holds for their control of organizations, both in economic and other spheres. Since, in any society, several forms of regulation tend to be mixed, it is best to review first the various analytical possibilities. At one extreme is the laissez-faire ideology associated with the traditional, liberal conception of the state. Here the state is expected to refrain from interfering in the relationships among organizations unless absolutely necessary, and mainly to avoid major public injury, such as that resulting from a long interruption of public services because of conflict between union and management, or between rival unions. Next there is the state which actively regulates a much larger variety of organizational interaction, including that between financial and productive organizations (e.g., in the stock exchange), among schools (regional registration), between political parties and mass media (e.g., equal time on the air), between schools and churches (to enforce separation), and so on. Third is the system of "indicative planning" in which the state provides a list

organization and the social environment

of economic goals which are likely to gain governmental support in future years. The state roughly divides new tasks among various organizational sectors, without directly controlling or compelling any one organization to follow the "indications." [6] Finally, there is the totalistic planned system, in which most of the organizations are subordinated directly to the state and receive specific orders from superior state organizations. Those, in turn, are under the control of one organization—the party.

The interaction of organizations in any one society is never regulated exclusively by any one pattern. The societal needs are too varied to allow even the most totalitarian society to mold all its organizational interactions into one pattern. Societies differ from one another in the kinds of combinations they form from the various analytical patterns. In general, the laissez-faire pattern is least heeded. It was never consistently imposed. No modern society relies on it to any significant extent in its relations with its organizations. Some sectors of all societies, in particular the public ones, are highly regulated. There is a general tendency for the public organization to grow; hence the scope of direct government control increases. It is important to realize that this increase in regulation has occurred not only in the relations among business firms or in economic matters but also among other organizations and in other matters. The relationship among the three American military services has become more regulated over the last two decades than it was before; new laws—especially the Taft-Hartley Act and the National Labor Relations Act—have increased governmental regulation of the relations between unions and corporations. The government's role in schools and hospitals has also grown.

The United States differs from most other countries in the size of the sector of organizational interaction which is comparatively free of control or government regulation. The scope of regulation is considerably higher in Britain, where some industries are nationalized and schools and hospitals are subject to much greater public control. In France, the home of indicative planning, organizational interaction is more highly regulated than in Britain. Communist societies maintain the most control over organization relations but even their organizations are less subject to governmental regulation than many outsiders believe. To some extent inter-organizational power plays characterize the relations between the party and the military, between the military and the various security services, between industrial management and labor organizations which have some freedom to bargain collectively about wages.[7] Moreover, in Communist societies there are sectors in agriculture, small business, and service industries which, although regulated, are not directly controlled.

To the degree that the relationship between any two organizations in any society is not ordered by a superior organization or regulated by a legal framework (e.g., anti-trust laws in the United States), the actual pattern of interaction is determined in the processes of exchange, conflict or coopera-

[6] This system has been employed in post-war France and is now used by the authorities of the European Common Market.

[7] See David Granick, *Management of the Industrial Firm in the U.S.S.R.* (New York: Columbia University Press, 1954).

tion, or bargaining, all of which are affected by ecological, cultural, and power factors.

Take, for example, the relationship between the police department and welfare agencies in major American cities. In part, their relations are determined by ecological factors—for instance, by the degree to which the police and the welfare agencies concentrate their efforts in the same area. The larger the ecological contact, the higher the need for patterning the interaction. The general cultural "tone" is another important factor affecting organizational interaction; in general, especially over recent decades, the public has tended to accept more and more the philosophy held by the social welfare agencies regarding the treatment of juvenile delinquents (though not of drug addicts) and less the traditional police approach. In cases of conflict, the press, public, and to a degree the politicians tend to side with the welfare agencies, a fact which affects the relationships between the two organizations. Their respective power in terms of their relations to political machines and political parties and their financial stability also affect their tendencies toward cooperation or conflict and the outcome of these tendencies. A strong police department in a major East Coast city largely disregards the demands and proposals of the welfare agencies and insists on a "tough line" with delinquents, whereas in a West Coast city with strong welfare agencies the police department has adopted many social-work procedures, and routinely turns juvenile delinquents over to the welfare agencies for treatment.

Among the empirical ways to assess the relative power of interacting organizations (none of which has been proven a reliable measure) is to establish the level at which the interaction occurs. Are the organizational representatives of the same rank or is one higher than the other? Which organization has greater control over shared facilities and projects? Which provides a larger share of the financing for shared activities?

Finally, no study of organizational interaction is complete until there is extensive study of the various bodies in which different organizational representatives regularly meet to coordinate their work. A large variety of ad hoc or permanent committees, councils, liaison officers, and second-order organizations have developed to coordinate the work of various organizations and to institutionalize their interaction. The National Security Council, in which representatives of government agencies meet to work out a shared security policy for the United States, illustrates the large number of malfunctions that arise in this type of structure, especially the tendency to mix strategies rather than come out in favor of any one.[8]

Organizational study has a long way to go before it will do justice to the crucial question of the organization of organizations. The importance of this problem should not be underestimated. Modern society is composed more and more of larger and larger organizations. Society has long recognized that it cannot leave economic interaction to the free play of market forces because this might not lead these organizations to pursue a course that will

[8] S. P. Huntington, *The Soldier and the State: The Theory and Politics of Civil-Military Relations* (Cambridge: Harvard University Press, 1957); and Arthur Waskow, *The Limits of Defense* (New York: Doubleday, 1962). See also Amitai Etzioni, *The Hard Way to Peace* (New York: Collier Books, 1962) Chap. 1.

organization and the social environment

bring the greatest happiness to the greatest number. The same holds for inter-action among organizations that do not pursue economic goals, and for the non-economic interactions of economic organizations. Modern society has found it necessary to build more and more instruments to regulate this inter-action to encourage increase not only in the effectiveness and satisfaction within each one but also of the relations among them.

Future Trends
of Organizational Societies

Trends in Less-developed Societies

There is a small but rapidly growing body of infor-mation on the emergence of organizations in the less-developed countries. The differences among these countries are enormous, and without a detailed discussion of their various social structures and cultures, which is outside the scope of this volume, there is little room for fruitful discussion. The most important general statement that can be made is that most of these countries are less differentiated, less "worldly" in their orientations, and less ascetic than the Western ones, and that the typical citizen is more oriented to short-run gratifications than to long-run ones, and is less achievement-oriented. While many of these societies have shown a growing appetite for the goods and services that efficient and effective modern organizations can provide, in few of them has there developed the intense commitment to the kind of behavior rational organization requires.

At one extreme are those traditional societies where an absolute mon-archy or a tight feudal system still prevails. Here there is little differentiation of structure in servicing various societal needs. Almost all functions are served by the extended family, the tribe, or the village community, under the au-thority of a single chief and a small group of his kin or supporters. Yemen is such a society. There are transitional societies which have a partially dif-ferentiated structure and some nation-wide organization. Here communica-tion and transportation, military enterprises, and some economic exchange is directed by a government bureaucracy from a few large urban centers. The bulk of the population, which is rural, is to be found in largely traditional communities. India is a prime example.

The societies closest to a modern one are those in which the nation-wide organizational web penetrates deeper into the societal structure, down to the villages, and voluntary associations develop in which citizens can pursue more of their ends independent of the state or government. Otherwise com-paratively developed countries, such as Argentina, are only now entering this phase.

The general trend in less-developed societies is toward more dif-ferentiation and the establishment of a greater number and larger variety of more encompassing organizations. Since it is quite possible to establish or-ganizations even when many of the cultural and psychological prerequisites of effective organizational behavior are not present, we are not surprised to find in these countries an unusually large variety of organizational ills includ-ing corruption (the use of organizational means to serve private goals);

113

nepotism and favoritism (in which preference is given to relatives and friends, and to one's political commitments over adherence to the bureaucratic criteria); bribery (in which organizational performance is directed by rewards given by private parties rather than by the organization); and simple inefficiency due to such things as ignorance, lack of motivation, lack of facilities, and poor coordination.

Sporadic efforts to eliminate these ills and to increase technical competence are as a rule limited in their effects because they focus on the symptoms rather than on the root of the matter. The source of the ills can be eliminated only by changing the culture and education of the participants and hence their psychological make-up, which is a long process. Organizational reforms seem to be successful at a late stage in the modernization process. Not until the second half of the nineteenth century, when the Industrial Revolution was three generations old, did the major organizational reforms of civil service take root in Britain. In the United States, reduction of organizational ills such as the "spoils system" and the professionalization of the governmental services were initiated only two generations or so after industrialization took place, and are still a long way from completion. Similarly, it is likely that a major increase in the effectiveness and efficiency of organizations in most developing countries will not come about in the foreseeable future. Furthermore it is quite possible for even a fairly modern society to function for many decades without a web of effective and efficient organizations. For example, anyone familiar with the Middle East will realize that graft can become so institutionalized that it becomes a way to run a factory, a school, an army. Such organizations, to be sure, have a much lower rationality than the bureaucratic model provides for, but they are not "impossible" modes of production, teaching, and fighting. Perhaps the level of efficiency attained is often not much lower than that which the particular society can carry, given its culture and its educational system. Large investments in organizational reforms are, under these circumstances, largely wasted.

Trends in Totalitarian Societies

In the initial post-revolutionary and highly charismatic phase, these societies tend to reduce differentiation not, as the popular image has it, by merging all the organizations into one huge bureaucracy that carries out all the various societal functions but by subordinating most organizations to centralized governmental control from without, and by controlling them from within to assure compliance to orders from above. Labor unions, corporations, cultural societies, and schools are controlled by the state from above and by the party from within. Still, each organization is an entity unto itself, with limited room for inter-organizational conflict and coalition.

The long-run trend, although not a linear one, is to increase the autonomy of the various organizations and, to some degree, the power play between them. To some extent, control by regulation (i.e., by setting limits) replaces control by decree (i.e., by specific orders). The amount of red tape and bureaucratic overhead required by control by decree is gigantic; the loss of effectiveness and efficiency is high. Young and ambitious groups can more readily be absorbed and the general alienation of the lower-in-rank can be

organization and the social environment

reduced by the granting of some local and organizational autonomy. If, for instance, the labor unions are completely subordinated to managerial requirements as determined by the state and industry, they cannot fulfill their functions as absorbers of protest. If, on the other hand, they are granted some autonomy in negotiations over wages, though, let us say, the final wage set cannot differ by more than 10 per cent from the rate set by the central planning agency, there is some place for bargaining between the factory and the union, and the union can to some degree fulfill its draining function. Soviet society seems to be moving in that direction.

Finally, the cultural and sociological changes occurring in other sectors of these societies work in the same direction, toward liberalization. How far this trend can proceed is impossible to forecast. Some believe that it will go all the way and create an organizational interaction pattern similar to the Western one, although somewhat more regulated (even the Western pattern is becoming more regulated); others believe the liberalization of these societies is a temporary phenomenon to be followed by a period of increased centralized control; and there are a variety of positions that fall between these two, such as the expectation that some additional liberalization might occur, or that regression will be limited.

A quite different question, often discussed in ideological terms, on which there is no conclusive evidence, is that of the comparative efficiency of organizations in such a context and their human cost. The Western observer tends to expect organizations in totalitarian societies to be either extremely inefficient (often pointing to the Russian Intourist organization), or inhumanly efficient (often pointing to the Russian space program). In either case, the human cost of totalitarian organization is believed to be high. In the first case, it is believed to be the source of inefficiency; in the second, the consequence of ultra-efficiency. Actually there is little hard evidence about these matters other than the fact that persons who have grown up in these societies view the costs differently from outsiders, and that both efficiency and human costs might vary considerably from organization to organization in these societies, as they do in Western societies.

Trends in Modern Democratic Societies

The trend in modern democratic societies, especially in the United States, has been to try to find a new balance between the organizational demands placed on participants and their personal and extra-organizational needs. As Riesman and Whyte point out, the tendency is to place a lesser, though still high, emphasis on organizational demands.[9] Executives take less work home; younger people prefer security to mobility within the organization, especially if promotion requires greater efforts and higher risks; workers are concerned with shorter hours, not just higher pay.

Within the organization, social and personal considerations have gained in importance, as compared to the traditional concern for production and administrative efficiency. It is thought important for the staff to be socially

[9] David Riesman, Nathan Glazer, and R. Denney, *The Lonely Crowd* (Garden City, N.Y.: Doubleday, 1955); and William H. Whyte, Jr., *The Organization Man* (Garden City, N.Y.: Doubleday, 1957).

compatible as well as a good work team. The wife is interviewed as well as the husband when he is being considered for a new position. To be sure, much of this emphasis on compatibility and conformity is designed to increase organizational efficiency, but it cannot help but affect social relations in the organization. Whatever judgment one might pass on this trend, there is little doubt that the rewards of the conformist have increased, for the organization both rewards his conformity and contributes to his social life. However, it is possible that the organization loses in efficiency because of the loss in initiative, innovative spirit, and achievement orientation, which results from the accent on harmony and social relations on the job.

Riesman's analysis of the organizational society and Whyte's observations on the organization man were made before the first Russian satellites were launched in late 1957. Since that time, with the intensification of competition between the United States and the U.S.S.R., there has been a general revival of concern with achievement and innovation in many organizations. Schools and colleges pay more attention to teaching mathematics and foreign languages than to producing well-rounded personalities that will fit readily into organizational and suburban "pigeonholes." Social activities, from coffee breaks to Christmas parties, have been curtailed in many industries. The nature of the new balance between the organization's needs and those of the participants (in part compatible) to be established in modern democratic societies in the next few years will be largely determined by developments beyond the control of any single society—by developments in the interaction among societies. The study of the environment of organizations must hence include both the national and the international settings.

organization and the social environment

selected references

While the following references are by no means comprehensive, they are an indication of the extent of the writings on organizations for those who seek a working background in the field.

In *Interpersonal Competence and Organizational Effectiveness* (Homewood, Ill.: The Dorsey Press, 1962), C. Argyris is one of the few authors who combines psychoanalytical with administrative perspectives. He draws largely on industrial data, and the resulting "mix" is applicable to organizational analysis in general. A classic that outlines the foundation of organizational analysis as seen a generation ago is C.I. Barnard, *The Functions of the Executive* (Cambridge: Harvard University Press, 1938). P.M. Blau, *The Dynamics of Bureaucracy* (Chicago: The University of Chicago Press, 1955) deals with a sociological study of social workers in two agencies and their relationships to their clientele and each other, highlighting the full significance of the theoretical implications of the data. W. Brown, a British executive influenced by the Human Relations School, relates his own experience in *Exploration in Management* (New York, Wiley, 1960). D. Cartwright and A. Zander (eds.), *Group Dynamics* (Evanston, Ill.: Row, Peterson, 1953) presents a selection of articles representing various social-psychological and psychological aspects of organizational analysis, including many articles written in the Human Relations tradition.

A highly readable, but largely descriptive, sociological study of real people running real corporations is M. Dalton, *Men Who Manage* (New York: Wiley, 1959). Written with a business school perspective, P.F. Drucker, *The Practice of Management* (New York: Harper, 1954) includes illustrative material demonstrating the way Sears, Ford, and IBM are managed. A large number of selections dealing briefly with many aspects of organizational life are dealt with in R. Dubin, *Human Relations in Administration* (Englewood Cliffs, N.J.: Prentice-Hall, 1951). A. Etzioni, *A Comparative Analysis of Complex Organizations* (Glencoe, Ill.: The Free Press, 1961) is a comparative study of a great variety of organizational types (armies, churches, corporations, hospitals, schools, and others) examined from a score of sociological dimensions. A selection of a few classical, largely recent, contributions to the study of organizational goals, structure, environment, and research methods is represented in A. Etzioni (ed.), *Complex Organizations: A Sociological Reader* (New York: Holt, Rinehart and Winston, 1961). The best organizational study of an American church is J.H. Fichter, *Social Relations in the Urban Parish* (Chicago: The University of Chicago Press, 1954).

R.A. Gordon, *Business Leadership in the Large Corporation* (Washington, D.C.: The Brookings Institute, 1945) discusses from an economist's viewpoint matters which other books listed here discuss from sociological or psychological viewpoints. A sociological case study of a gypsum mine and its implication for Weber's theory form the central focus for A.W. Gouldner, *Patterns of Industrial Bureaucracy* (Glencoe, Ill.: The Free Press, 1954). D.E. Griffiths in his *Administrative Theory* (New York: Appleton-Century-Crofts, 1959) is representative of the classical-administrative approach writing from a teacher-college vantage point. M. Haire, *Psychology in Management* (New York: McGraw-Hill, 1956) is a textbook which approaches organizations from a Human Relations perspective. M. Janowitz, *Sociology and the Military Establishment* (New York: Russell Sage Foundation, 1959) is considered the best sociological overview of military organizations, with special attention to the American ones.

Human Relations ideas are supported by survey data in D. Katz, N. Maccoby, G. Gurin, and Lucretia G. Floor, *Productivity Supervision and Morale among Railroad Workers* (Ann Arbor: Survey Research Center, University of Michigan, 1951). S.M. Lipset, M.A. Trow, and J.S. Coleman, *Union Democracy* (Glencoe, Ill.: The Free Press, 1956) provides a rare, successful marriage of sociological data with sociological theory, which has much to offer to the politically and intellectually curious. Of importance for advanced students is J.G. March and H. Simon, *Organizations* (New York: Wiley, 1958). R.K. Merton, Ailsa P. Gray, Barbara Hockey, and H.C. Selvin (eds.), *Reader in Bureaucracy* (Glencoe, Ill.: The Free Press, 1952) presents a collection of excerpts from Weber's work, works conducted under his influence, or works extending his insights into the study of bureaucracy.

A textbook of administrative gender written from a business school perspective is W.H. Newman, *Administrative Action: The Techniques of Organization and Management* (Englewood Cliffs, N.J.: Prentice-Hall, 1951). In *TVA and the Grass Roots* (Berkeley: University of California, 1953), P. Selznick provides a case study of the relationship between government agencies and the people they set out to serve. A sociological study of a maximum security prison, with an effective postscript for social reformers, is presented by G.M. Sykes, *The Society of Captives* (Princeton: Princeton University Press, 1958). P.D. Thompson, P.B. Hammond, R.W. Hawkes, B.H. Junker, and A. Tuden (eds.), *Comparative Studies in Administration* (Pittsburgh: University of Pittsburgh Press, 1959) includes a collection of articles on organizations in several cultural settings by anthropologists, psychologists, and sociologists. A comparison of the organization of work in many so-called primitive societies, S.H. Udy, Jr., *Organization of Work: A Comparative Analysis of Production among Nonindustrial Peoples* (New Haven: HRAF, 1959a) provides a meticulous analysis of data that varies largely in quality.

selected references

index

120

index